Science That's Appropriate <u>and</u> Doable

This science resource book was written with two goals in mind:

- to provide "good" science for your students
- to make it easy for you

What makes this book "good" science?

When you follow the step-by-step lessons in this book, you'll be using an instructional model that makes science education relevant to real life.

- Your students will be drawn in by interesting activities that encourage them to express what they already know about a concept.

- Your students will participate in hands-on discovery experiences and be guided to describe the experiences in their own words. Together, you'll record the experiences in both class and individual logbooks.

- You'll provide explanations and vocabulary that will help your students accurately explain what they have experienced.

- Your students will have opportunities to apply their new understandings to new situations.

What makes this book easy for you?

- The step-by-step activities are easy to understand and have illustrations where it's important.

- The resources you need are at your fingertips—record sheets; logbook forms; and other reproducibles such as mini-books, task cards, picture cards, and pages to make into overhead transparencies.

- Each science concept is presented in a self-contained section. You can decide to do the entire book or pick only those sections that enhance your own curriculum.

> For sites on the World Wide Web that supplement the material in this resource book, go to http://www.evan-moor.com and look for the <u>Product Updates</u> link on the main page.

Using Logbooks as Learning Tools

Logbooks are valuable learning tools for several reasons:
- Logbooks give students an opportunity to put what they are learning into their own words.
- Putting ideas into words is an important step in internalizing new information. Whether spoken or written, this experience allows students to synthesize their thinking.
- Explaining and describing experiences help students make connections between several concepts and ideas.
- Logbook entries allow the teacher to catch misunderstandings right away and then reteach.
- Logbooks are a useful reference for students and a record of what has been learned.

Two Types of Logbooks

The Class Logbook

A class logbook is completed by the teacher and the class together. The teacher records student experiences and helps students make sense of their observations. The class logbook is a working document. You will return to it often for a review of what has been learned. As new information is acquired, make additions and corrections to the logbook.

Individual Science Logbooks

Individual students process their own understanding of investigations by writing their own responses in their own logbooks. Two types of logbook pages are provided in this unit.

1. Open-ended logbook pages:
   Pages 4 and 5 provide two choices of pages that can be used to respond to activities in the unit. At times you may wish students to write in their own logbooks and then share their ideas as the class logbook entry is made. After the class logbook has been completed, allow students to revise and add information to their own logbooks. At other times you may wish students to copy the class logbook entry into their own logbooks.

2. Specific logbook pages:
   You will find record forms or activity sheets following many activities that can be added to each student's logbook.

At the conclusion of the unit, reproduce a copy of the logbook cover on page 3 for each student. Students can then organize both types of pages and staple them with the cover.

How My Body Works

_____
Name

How Your Body Works • EMC 856

Note: Reproduce this form for students to record knowledge gained from daily science lessons.

Name ______________________________

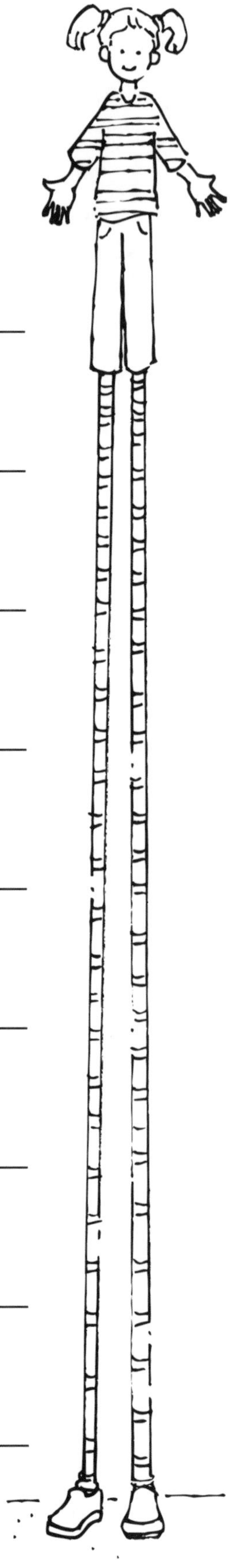

This is what I learned about my body today:

____

____

____

____

____

____

____

____

____

Note: Reproduce this form for students to record science investigations for their individual logs.

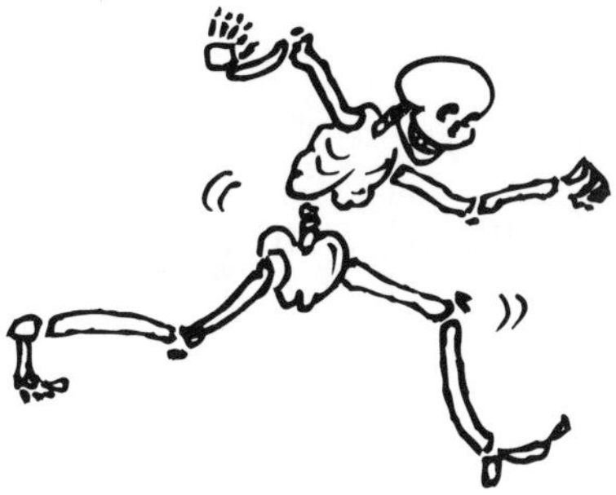

Name ____________________

Investigation: ____________________

____

What we did:

____

____

____

What we saw:

____

____

____

What we learned:

____

____

____

Bodies change as they grow older.

Teaching Resources

- Before beginning the activities, set up an area in the classroom with books, picture cards, puzzles, and models for students to explore throughout this unit of study.

- Check your school and public library for appropriate materials.

- Check to see what types of videos on the human body are available in your school district. Show these where appropriate in the unit.

How Have We Changed?

- Share a picture of yourself as a baby with the class. Have students describe how you have changed as you've grown older. List these changes on the chalkboard. Ask students to predict how you will change as you continue to age. Add these changes to the list. Leave the list posted in the classroom as you continue studying this concept.

Teacher Then
He was little.
He didn't have any hair.
He didn't have any teeth.
His feet were little.

Teacher Now
He is big.
He has a moustache.
He has big feet.
His hair is long.

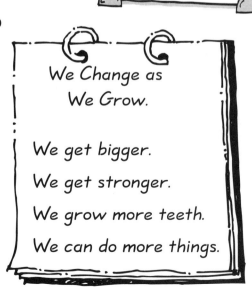

- Reproduce the questionnaire on page 9 for each student to take home.

- After the questionnaires are returned, allow students time to share what they learned about how they have changed. Record changes on the chalkboard. Identify and circle the changes that were common to everyone.

- Begin your class log for the unit with a page entitled "We Change as We Grow." Record the changes circled on the chalkboard. Have students write about changes in their individual logs, using the form on page 4.

We Change as We Grow.

We get bigger.

We get stronger.

We grow more teeth.

We can do more things.

A Book about Me

Have students use the information they learned about themselves from the homework activity to make individual accordion books showing several stages of growth.

Materials

- 6″ x 18″ (15 cm x 45.5 cm) piece of construction paper
- crayons
- pencil

Steps to Follow

1. Guide students to fold the paper.

a.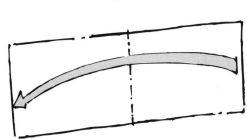
b.
c.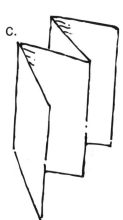

2. Have students create a cover on the first page.

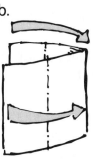

My Life
by
_____
name

3. Have students write one sentence on each page and illustrate the sentence.

I was a little baby. 1

When I was two I had teeth and hair. 2

When I was four I rode a trike. 3

I am seven now. I lost three teeth I can read. 4

Human Life Cycles

- Explain that the changes people go through are part of a cycle. People are born, grow up, have babies, and die. This happens over and over again. Make a new class log entry entitled "Cycles." Ask students to tell what they think a cycle is. Write this on the chart paper. Explain that they have written a meaning for a cycle and that this meaning is called a definition. Reproduce page 4 for each student. Have them write the definition for their individual logs.

- Reproduce page 10 for each student. They are to write a sentence about each stage of the human life cycle.

- Start individual growth-record booklets. Reproduce six copies of page 11 for each student. Cut the pages in half and staple them between a construction paper cover. Measure and weigh everyone. The students are to write the results on the first page of their booklets. Have students help each other measure the head, one hand, and one foot and record these measurements. Take all the measurements again at the end of each month to verify growth. At the end of the school year, send the booklets home with students. Any unused pages can be completed at home.

Other Life Cycles

- Explain that not just people have a life cycle. Ask students to think of other living things they know about that change as they grow.

- Make an overhead transparency of page 12. Show this to students as you discuss the changes that occur in the life cycle of a plant or an animal.

- Check your school library and audiovisual catalog for books and videos that show the life cycle of a plant or an animal. Share these with your students, then compare the human life cycle with that of a plant or an animal. List the characteristics that are common to all of the cycles (birth, growth, reproduction, and death).

Name_____

Dear Parents,
Our class is learning about how we change as we grow older.
Please help your child complete this form.
If you have photographs you do not mind sharing, return them with
the form by _____ .

When I was born...

I weighed: _____ .

I was: _____ long.

What I looked like: _____

_____ .

What I could do:_____

_____ .

This is how I had changed when I was two.

What I looked like: _____

_____

_____ .

What I could do: _____

_____

_____ .

This is how I had changed when I was four.

What I looked like: _____

_____

_____ .

What I could do: _____

_____

_____ .

This is me now.

What I look like: _____

_____

_____ .

What I can do: _____

_____

_____ .

Note: Reproduce this page for each student to use with page 8.

Name_____

Human Life Cycle

1. _____

_____

2. _____

_____

3. _____

_____

4. _____

_____

5. _____

_____

6. _____

_____

Note: Reproduce six copies of this form for each student to use with page 8.

Name_____ Date_____

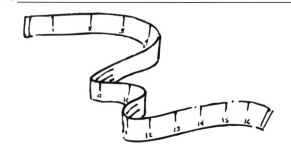

This is what I look like:

I am_____ tall.

I weigh _____ .

My head is _____ around.

My hand is _____ long.

My foot is _____ long.

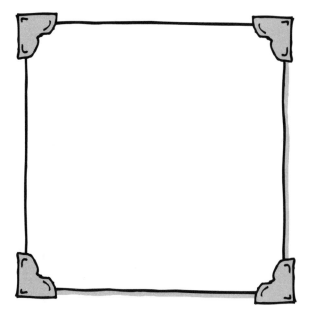

11

- -

Name_____ Date_____

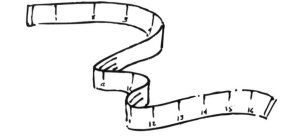

This is what I look like:

I am_____ tall.

I weigh _____ .

My head is _____ around.

My hand is _____ long.

My foot is _____ long.

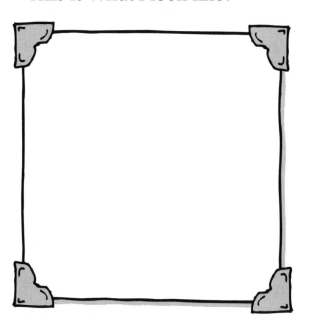

Life Cycles

flower

dog

frog

How Your Body Works • EMC 856

The body has external and internal parts.

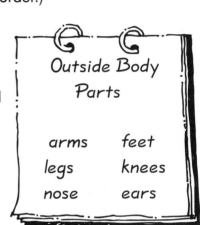

My Body Parts

- Divide the class into small groups. Each group is to brainstorm to create a list of as many body part names as they can in five minutes. One person in each group acts as the recorder. (You may need an adult helper or a cross-age tutor to act as recorder.)

Call the groups together to share their lists. Write the composite list on a chart. (Save the list for a later activity.) After each group has shared, examine the list together asking, "Is this body part on the outside or inside of your body?" Circle "outside" parts and underline "inside" parts.

- Create a page for the class log entitled "Outside Body Parts." Add new words to the list later. Have students write in their individual logs, using the form on page 4.

Outside Body Parts

arms	feet
legs	knees
nose	ears

Collage People

Make collage people by cutting pictures of body parts from magazines.

Materials
- construction paper 12" x 18" (30.5 x 45.5 cm)
- a large assortment of magazines with colorful photos and illustrations
- scissors
- paste
- black marking pen

Steps to Follow

1. Explain to students that they are going to make a human body by cutting out pieces from pictures and pasting the parts together. They are to use no more than two parts from the same picture. (Have groups of students share stacks of magazines.)

2. Students cut and paste until they have a completed body.

3. They then label as many parts as they can.

Where Is It?

- Prepare students for this activity by adding to the list of external body parts started earlier. Ask students to think of body part names they may have forgotten earlier. As you write each word, ask students to show you where the part is on their bodies. If no one knows, point to the place on your own body.

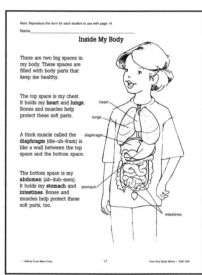

abdomen	crown	calf	wrist
armpit	earlobe	waist	buttocks
knuckle	thigh	palm	sole
chest	nostril	shin	ankle

- Play "Where Is It?" with the words on the list. Name a part and ask, "Where is it?" Have students locate that part on their own bodies.

Inside My Body

- Make an overhead transparency of page 16. Reproduce a copy of page 17 for each student. Explain that our "outside" parts cover and protect our "inside" parts. Show the transparency as you explain how the body is divided into two large parts separated by a "wall" of muscle (diaphragm) at the bottom of the rib cage. Have them identify the organs in the chest cavity (heart and lungs) and in the abdomen (stomach, intestines, etc.).

- Have students color page 17 and place it in their individual logs.

- Add a page entitled "Inside My Body" to the class log.

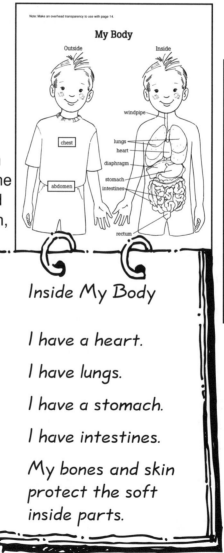

Inside My Body

I have a heart.

I have lungs.

I have a stomach.

I have intestines.

My bones and skin protect the soft inside parts.

Skin

- Engage students in a discussion of the large body organ that can be seen from the outside—skin.

1. Pass out magnifying glasses so students can take a close look at their skin. Ask them to describe what they see. (My skin has little holes in it. I see hair on my hands and arms. There are little lines on my fingers.)

2. Ask questions about skin. Provide as much additional information as is appropriate for the level of your students.

> "What covers your whole body?" *(skin)*
> "What are the jobs of skin?" *(It keeps dirt and germs out; it helps keep my body cool and warm enough; it helps me feel things.)*
> "Why do people have different colors of skin?" *(Skin has tiny bits of brown color called melanin. Skin with a lot of melanin is darker; skin with a little is lighter. Freckles are bits of melanin in clusters.)*
> "What parts of the skin can we see growing?" *(hair, fingernails, and toenails)*
> "Why can we feel things with our skin?" *(tiny nerve cells carry messages to the brain)*

- Work with students to add a page entitled "Skin" to the class log. Have students write about skin in their individual logs, using the form on page 4.

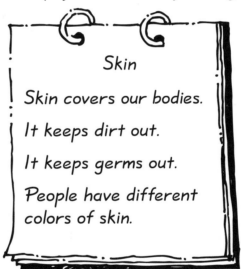

> Skin
>
> Skin covers our bodies.
>
> It keeps dirt out.
>
> It keeps germs out.
>
> People have different colors of skin.

Extension Activity—Fingerprints

- Have students take a close look at their fingertips with a magnifying glass. Explain that everyone has a different pattern of lines and swirls.

- Make a print of each student's thumb on a small file card. At the same time, put one thumb print for each student on a sheet of paper. Allow each student to take their thumb print card and try to match it to the correct print on the sheet of paper.

- Have students tape their fingerprint card in their individual log and write about what they've learned.

My Body

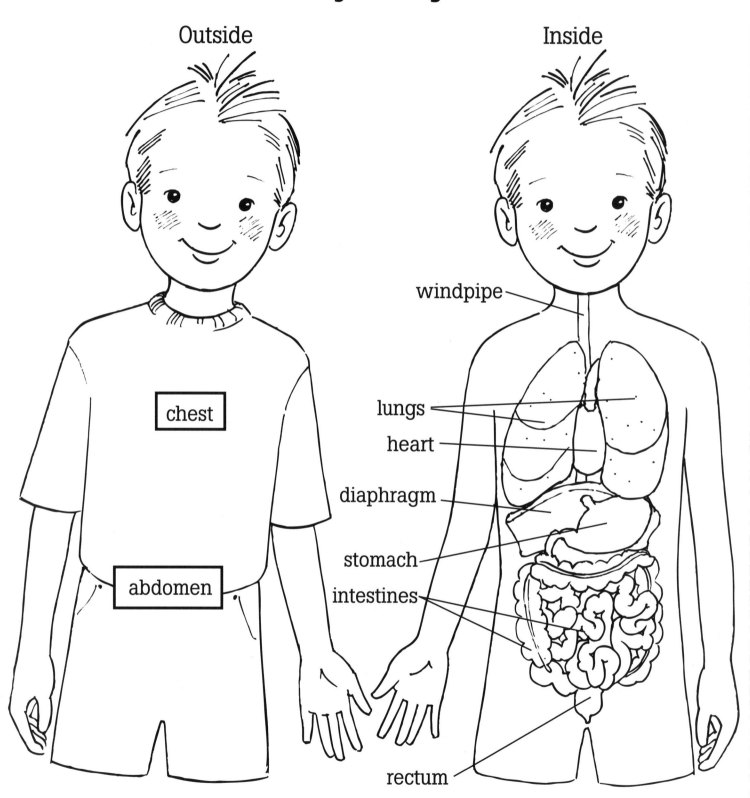

Outside

chest

abdomen

Inside

windpipe

lungs

heart

diaphragm

stomach

intestines

rectum

Name_____

Inside My Body

There are two big spaces in my body. These spaces are filled with body parts that keep me healthy.

The top space is my chest. It holds my **heart** and **lungs**. Bones and muscles help protect these soft parts.

A thick muscle called the **diaphragm** (die-uh-fram) is like a wall between the top space and the bottom space.

The bottom space is my **abdomen** (ab-duh-men). It holds my **stomach** and **intestines**. Bones and muscles help protect these soft parts, too.

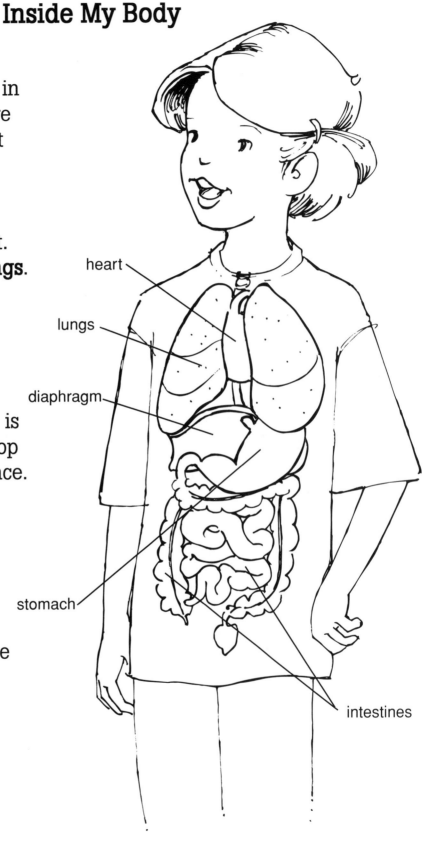

heart

lungs

diaphragm

stomach

intestines

17   How Your Body Works • EMC 856

The brain controls the body and is the center of thinking.

The Body's Control Center

• Engage students in a discussion of what controls our movements and memory. Begin by giving a series of directions for students to follow.

"Touch the top of your head with your left hand."
"Now make a funny face."
"Stand up and then sit back down."
"Sit quietly for a moment."

• Ask, "How does your body know how to do these things?" Record their ideas on a class log page entitled "How My Body Knows What to Do." Misconceptions will be corrected later as students learn more about how the brain works.

> **How My Body Knows What to Do**
>
> It just knows what to do.
>
> When I think about what I want to do, my body does it.
>
> My brain tells me what to do.

What My Brain Does

• Read *It's All In Your Brain* by Joy Ingram and Sylvia Funston (Grosset & Dunlap, 1995).

• Ask students to recall what they learned about what the brain does and how it works from listening to the story. Record their new knowledge about the brain in the class logbook on a page entitled "My Brain." Students will use copies of page 4 to write about the brain for their individual logs.

> **My Brain**
>
> My eyes, ears, nose, and skin send messages to my brain.
>
> Nerves carry the messages.
>
> Then my brain sends messages to all parts of my body.
>
> The messages tell my body what to do.
>
> My brain helps me learn how to do new things, too.

Parts of the Brain

Use a model of the brain if one is available or make an overhead transparency of page 20. Reproduce a copy for each student to color for their individual logs.

Point out the areas of the brain and what each area does. (It isn't necessary for students to be able to name the areas, just that they be aware that different areas have different functions.)

cerebrum—hear, smell, touch, talk, move, think
cerebellum—coordination and balance
brain stem—automatic functions such as breathing, heartbeat, etc.

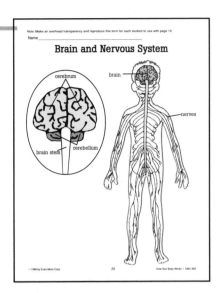

My Brain Mini-book

Reprodu ... 21 and 22 for each student.
Read an ... hat has been
learned. ... nd individual logs.

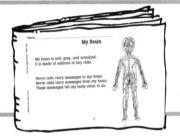

Extension

• Make a ...

Ask stud ... sages get to and from the brain. After listening to their
explana ... and sends information using nerve cells.
Explain ... cells in our body. Show the transparency of different
types of ... ormation. Point to each type of cell as you mention it.

"Your body is made up of trillions of tiny cells. Different parts of your body have different kinds of cells. A scientist or doctor looking at cells under a microscope can tell if the cells come from the brain, lung, or heart.

"There are cells for different kinds of jobs. Nerve cells carry messages. Other cells build the parts of your body such as lungs, muscles, and bones. You have several kinds of cells in your blood, each with a different job.

"Your body is always changing as old cells die and new cells are made. Your body is a very busy place!"

• Write a page for the class log entitled "Cells." Have students write about cells in their individual logs using the form on page 4.

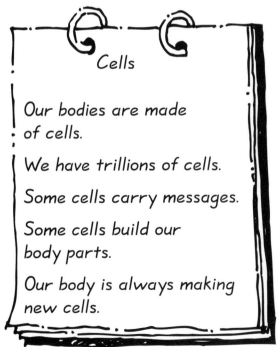

Cells

Our bodies are made of cells.

We have trillions of cells.

Some cells carry messages.

Some cells build our body parts.

Our body is always making new cells.

Name_____

Brain and Nervous System

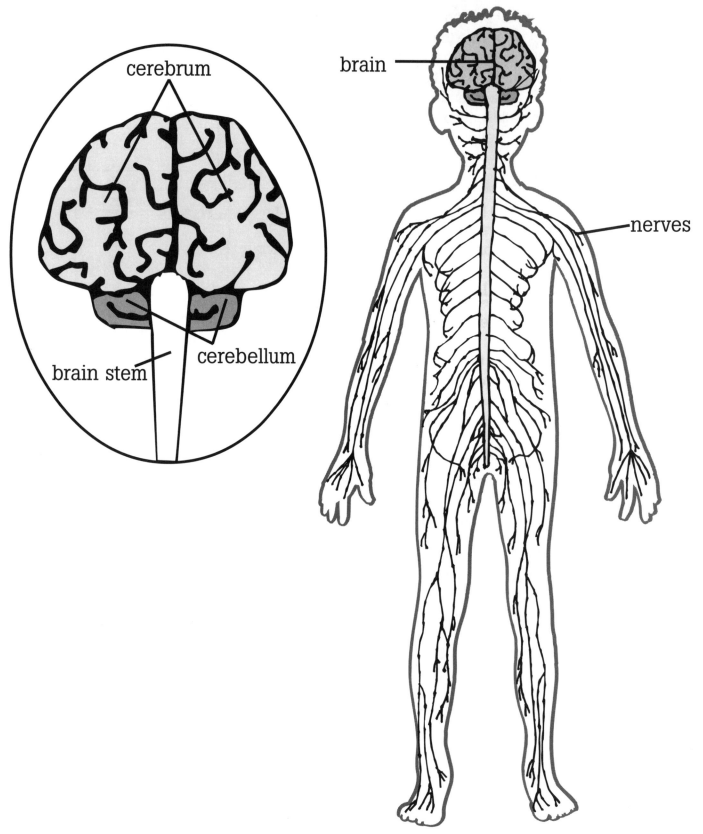

cerebrum

brain

brain stem

cerebellum

nerves

My Brain

My brain is soft, gray, and wrinkled.
It is made of millions of tiny cells.

Nerve cells carry messages to my brain.
Nerve cells carry messages from my brain.
These messages tell my body what to do.

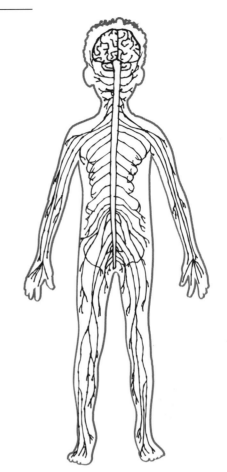

1

My brain has three parts.
I use part 1 whenever I see,
hear, touch, speak, or move
my muscles.

I use part 2 of my brain to
help me keep my balance.

Part 3 keeps my lungs
breathing and my
heart beating.

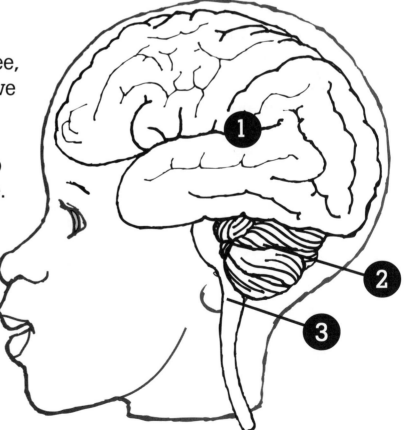

2

My brain lets me
remember things.
My brain lets me
learn new things.

3

My brain is protected
by a hard skull.
It is protected by a
layer of liquid, too.

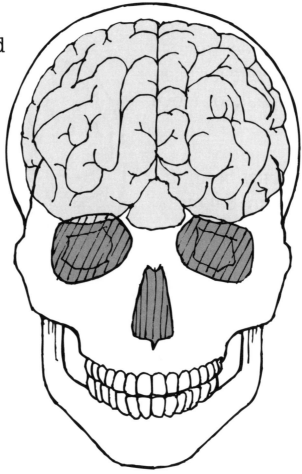

4

Cells

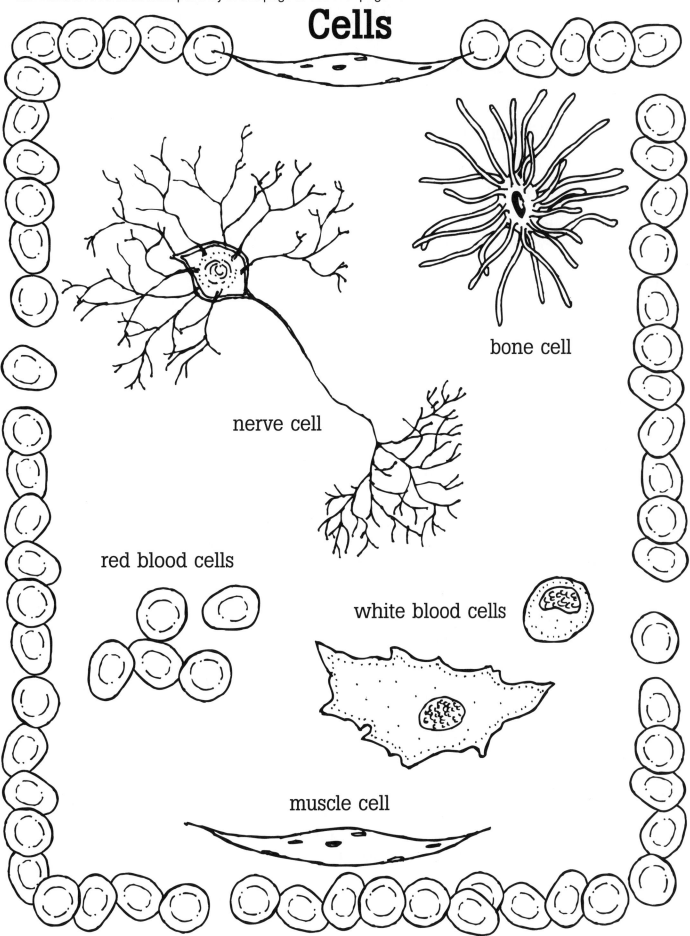

bone cell

nerve cell

red blood cells

white blood cells

muscle cell

How Your Body Works • EMC 856

We use five senses to find out about our world.

Preparation for Five Senses Activities

- Make an overhead transparency of page 31. Reproduce the mini-book on pages 32–37 for each student.

- Check your district audiovisual catalog for available filmstrips and videos on the topic of the five senses.

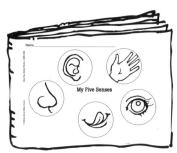

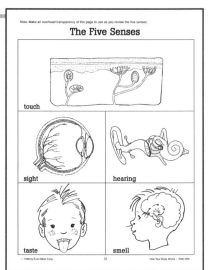

Five Senses Walk

- Take your class for a "senses" walk. Provide each student with a "clipboard" and a record sheet, set up as shown in the illustration. Students may use pictures or words to record what they see, hear, touch, and smell.

- Back in the classroom discuss what students observed using each of their senses. Record these on a sheet of butcher paper divided into five sections. Label the first four sections "smell," "see," "touch," and "hear."

- After recording what was observed in each of the labeled sections, ask, "Who can tell me the other sense we use every day?" (You may need to use a series of questions to help them reach "taste.") Have students give several examples of things they can taste. You will need to question students to get more than just "food" answers. Ask, "Have you ever tasted medicine? What did it taste like? Did you ever chew on a leaf, flower, or blade of grass? What did it taste like? Has anyone ever dared you to taste something strange? What was it? What did it taste like?"

- Have students write about what they learned on the walk in their individual logs, using the form on page 4.

Touch is one of the five senses.
Vocabulary of Touch

Have students sit in a circle. Pass around objects with different textures (feathers, satin, sandpaper, plastic wrap, wool, a piece of ice, bark, a metal spoon, etc.). As students describe what they are feeling, begin a list of descriptive words on chart paper or the chalkboard.

smooth	rough	soft	hard
bumpy	slick	cold	warm
sharp	itchy	fluffy	squishy

Mystery Box

• Take a box with a lid. Cut a hole in the side large enough for a hand to pass through. Place several items in the box. Call on a student to find the object you name using only the sense of touch. Ask the student to explain how the object was identified. Repeat several times with different students.

• Make the task more challenging:

1. Place objects of similar shape in the box (orange, grapefruit, rubber ball, ball of yarn, etc.).
2. Place coins of different values in the box.
3. Place two pieces each of several types of fabric. The student must find a pair.

Gather More Information

• Use the "touch" section of the overhead transparency (page 31) to show students the sensory cells that carry messages to the brain. (Cover the remaining pictures.)

• Read and complete pages 1 and 2 of the mini-book together.

• Show a video or filmstrip about touch or read appropriate sections from books on the senses. Have students recall what they have learned. Record their comments on the chalkboard.

Summary Activities

• Guide students in a discussion of the sense of touch. Ask them how touch helps them every day. To get them started, you may need to ask specific questions, such as, "How does touch help when you play ball?" or "How does touch keep you safe from harm in the kitchen?"

• Record learnings on a class log page entitled "Touch." Have students write about touch in their individual logs, using the form on page 4.

Taste is one of the five senses.
Name the Taste

- To help students understand the terms "salty," "bitter," "sour," and "sweet," gather these food items:

      potato chips (salty)
      unsweetened chocolate (bitter)
      dill pickle bits (sour)
      honey (sweet)

  One at a time, have student volunteers close their eyes and stick out their tongues. Drop a bit of food on the tongue. Ask, "What do you taste? Describe the taste."

- Divide the class into small groups, each with an adult helper, to give everyone a chance to identify sweet, sour, bitter, and salty tastes.

Materials

- foods to taste, numbered for identification:
      1. lemon juice (sour)   3. vanilla extract (bitter)
      2. sugar (sweet)   4. salt (salty)
- plastic spoons
- paper to record taste descriptions, numbered 1–4

Steps to Follow

1. Students in the group close their eyes.
2. The helper puts a small amount on each student's tongue and says, "This is taste number 1."
3. Ask each student to describe the taste. If they disagree, review what each taste word describes and repeat the test.
4. Record the name of the taste (sour, sweet, salty, bitter) next to its number.
5. Repeat with the other three samples.

Follow Up

- Bring the groups together and compare the test results. Share the identities of the foods tasted.

- Ask students to tell what they learned about the tongue and taste. *(My tongue can taste different tastes. The sour lemon taste made my mouth and eyes squeeze shut.)*

Gather More Information

- Use the "taste" section of the overhead transparency (page 31) as you review the sense of taste.
- Read and complete pages 3 and 4 of the mini-book together.
- Show a video or filmstrip about taste. Discuss what is learned.
- Record learnings on a class log page entitled "Taste." Have students write about taste for their individual logs, using the form on page 4.

Smell is one of the five senses.
Classroom Scents

- Have the students close their eyes as you spray perfume in the air. Ask students to tell what you have done and to explain how they know.

- Challenge the class to locate ten different smells in the classroom. Allow them two minutes to move around "sniffing" the room. Record their discoveries on the chalkboard.

Match the Smells

Make a set of "smell" jars ahead of time. Soak two cotton balls in each smell. Place one cotton ball in each jar. Put on the lids. (Code the jars so that you know which jars match.)
Use smells such as vanilla extract, lemon juice, pickle juice, perfume, ground nutmeg, and ground cinnamon.

Steps to Follow

1. Put one jar from each pair on a table. Reserve the other jar from each pair. You will hand these jars to students one at a time.
2. Call up a student to sit in a chair at the table and put on a blindfold.
3. Give the student one jar to smell. The student is to then smell the jars on the table until a match is made.
4. Continue the activity, following steps 2 and 3 with a new student each time.

Follow Up

After the smell test, ask students to explain what they learned about "smell." *(We smell with our nose. I could smell nice smells and sour smells. I can tell what something is by smelling it.)*

Gather More Information

- Use the "smell" section of the overhead transparency on page 31 to show students as you review the sense of smell.
- Read and complete pages 5 and 6 of the mini-book together.
- Show a video or filmstrip about smell. Have students recall what they have heard.
- Record learnings on a class log page entitled "Smell." Have students write about smell in their individual logs, using the form on page 4.

Summary Activity

Help students understand that smell and taste work together. Have a volunteer sit with closed eyes, tongue stuck out, and nose pinched shut as you place drops of orange juice, then lemon juice, on the tongue. Ask, "Did you taste one thing or two things?" "Without smell, it is difficult to tell. This is why things taste different when you have a cold."

Hearing is one of the five senses.
What Do You Hear?

Place several sound-making devices on a table (bell, drum, jar of rice, toy horn, whistle, etc.). Have a student sit in a chair with the student's back to the table. Make a sound with one of the items. Have the student try to name the item. Repeat the activity, selecting a new student each time.

Sound Jars

Prepare several pairs of unbreakable containers containing different items. Use beans, marbles, rice, cotton puffs, sand, toothpicks, etc. Reserve the other jar from each pair. You will hand these jars to students one at a time.

Steps to Follow

1. Seat a blindfolded student at the table.
2. Hand one jar from the reserved set to the student. Have the student shake the jar to hear the sound and then shake the other jars to find the matching sound.
3. Remove the blindfold so the student can verify that the two jars do match.
4. Repeat the activity several times with a different student each time.

Follow Up

After the sound test, have students describe the sounds they heard (*clink, tinkle, tap-tap, swish-swish, etc.*) Ask, "Could you tell what the objects were by the sounds they made?" (*I could tell the beans because I've heard beans shaking in a jar before. I knew the sand was something small, but I didn't know it was sand.*) Ask, "How do you know what is making a sound if you can't see it?" (*I know if it's something I've heard before, like a fire truck or my dog.*)

Gathering Information

• Show the "hearing" section of the overhead transparency on page 31 as you review the sense of hearing.
• Read and complete pages 7 and 8 of the mini-book together.
• Show a video or filmstrip about hearing. Have students recall what they have heard.
• Record learnings on a class log page entitled "Hearing." Have students write about hearing in their individual logs, using the form on page 4.

Sight is one of the five senses.
Using My Eyes

- Engage students in a discussion of the ways they use their eyes. Ask, "What are some of the ways we use our eyes?" *(read, watch television, recognize our friends, see where we are going).* Then use the following activity to demonstrate why sight is important.

- Clear an area in the classroom. Set a table and two chairs in different parts of the cleared area. Blindfold a student, turn the student around twice and say, "Walk to the table." (Remind the blindfolded student to walk slowly.) Ask the rest of the students to remain quiet as the blindfolded child moves around. Repeat with several students, asking each one to find one of the pieces of furniture.

- Ask the students who were blindfolded to explain how they felt as they tried to find their way. Have the rest of the students describe what they saw the blindfolded student do *(put arms out, slid feet along, tried to peek under the blindfold).*

Gather More Information

- Use the "sight" section of the overhead transparency on page 31 to show students as you review the sense of sight.

- Read and complete pages 9–11 of the mini-book together.

- Show a video or filmstrip about sight or read sections from reference books. Have students recall what they have heard.

- Record learnings on a class log page entitled "Sight." Have students write about sight in their individual logs, using the form on page 4.

Extension Activity—Pupils Change Size

Have students find a partner. Have the partners face each other.
1. Tell students to look at the black center of their partner's eyes.
2. Have one partner close his or her eyes while the other student counts to 30.
3. When the students have counted to 30, have the partner open his or her eyes and tell the other student to look at the black center again. Ask, "What do you see?" *(The pupils change size.)*

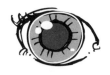

Explain that the center (pupil) gets bigger when there is little light and gets smaller when there is more light. Provide a mirror for students to watch their own pupils change size.

Review the Five Senses

- Now that all five senses have been introduced, ask students to help you write a definition of "Senses" for the class log.

- Read each of the class and individual log entries for the five senses. Make any changes, corrections, or additions to the logs.

- Reproduce pages 38 and 39 for each student.

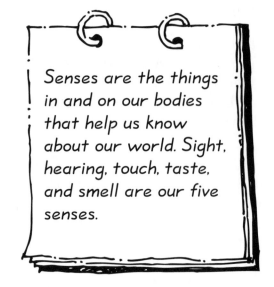

Senses are the things in and on our bodies that help us know about our world. Sight, hearing, touch, taste, and smell are our five senses.

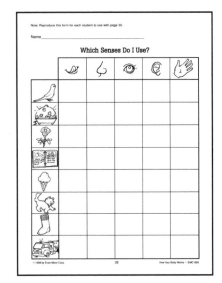

Students check the box under each sense they used to identify each item pictured.

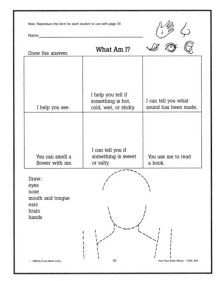

What Am I?—Students draw the item described and then complete the illustration.

The Five Senses

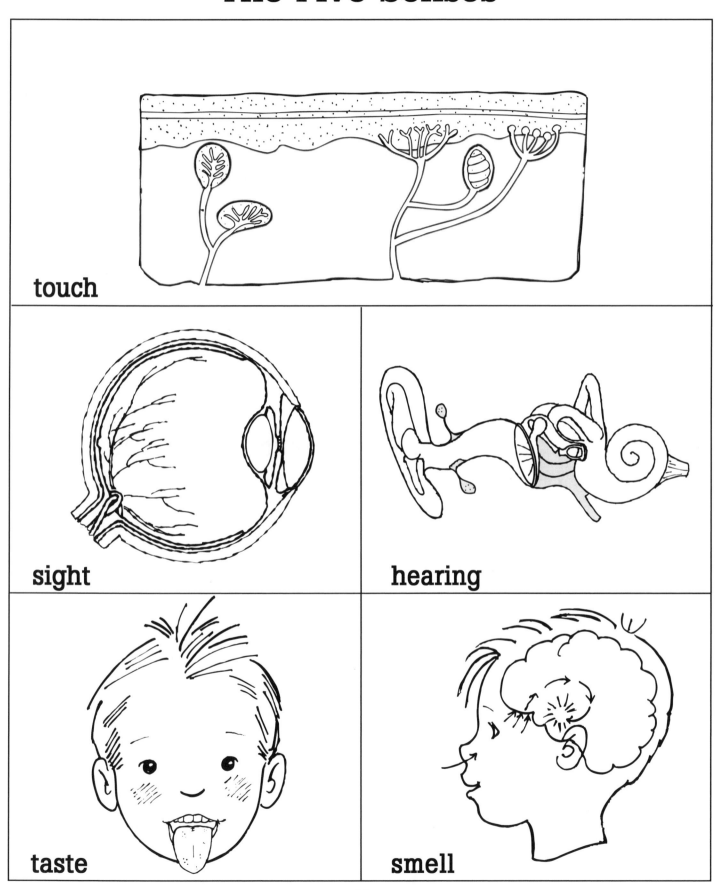

touch

sight

hearing

taste

smell

How Your Body Works • EMC 856

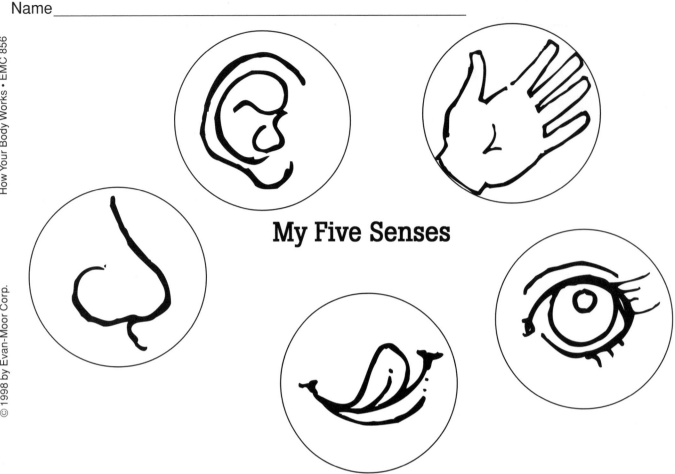

My Five Senses

- -

My Sense of Touch

The skin on my body is filled with little **nerve cells**. When I touch something with any part of my body, the little cells take messages to my brain. I have nerve cells for heat, cold, pressure, and pain.

I can tell if something is smooth or rough, soft or hard, wet or dry, or if it is hot or cold.

Some of my nerve cells warn me of danger by letting me feel pain.

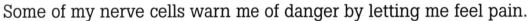
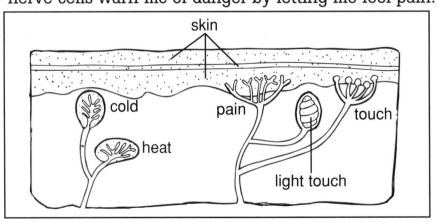

1

Match:

hot

cold

wet

dry

soft

hard

rough

smooth

2

My Sense of Taste

Little bumps on my tongue let me taste food.
These little bumps are called **taste buds**.
I have different kinds of taste buds on
different parts of my tongue.

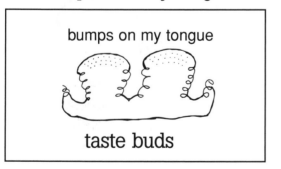

bumps on my tongue

taste buds

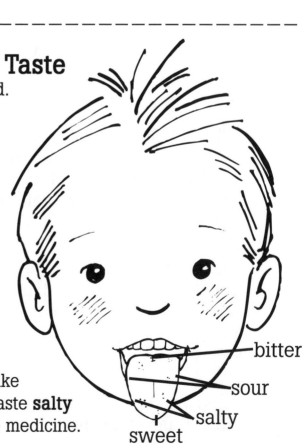

bitter

sour

salty

sweet

Some taste buds tell me if a food is **sweet** like
candy or **sour** like a lemon. Others let me taste **salty**
things like potato chips or **bitter** things like medicine.

The taste buds send information along nerves to my brain.
Then I can taste things.

3

When I taste my food, I smell it with my nose, too. I use my tongue to feel my food. I can tell if it is crisp, soft, smooth, or lumpy.

Draw:

sweet things	sour things	salty things

4

My Sense of Smell

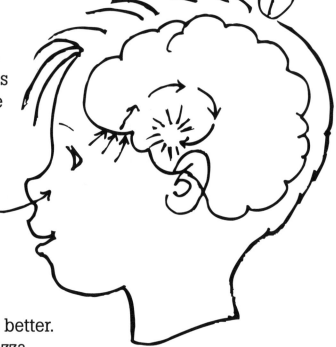

When I breathe, air comes into my **nose** through two holes called **nostrils**. Nerves carry information about the smells in the air from my nose to my brain. Then I can smell.

Sometimes the smell is really good. Sometimes it is really bad, like a skunk. Sometimes it protects me from danger. If I smell smoke, I know to look out for fire.

Being able to smell makes my food taste better. When I smell something delicious like pizza, I just have to eat it.

5

Match:

I collect smells with my	nerves
These let the air into my nose.	nose
These carry information about smells from my nose to my brain.	nostrils

Circle things that smell good. Put an X on things that smell bad.

6

My Sense of Hearing

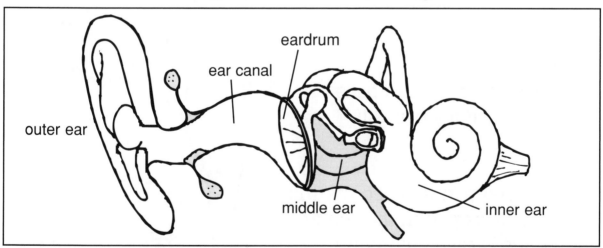

I hear with my ears. I hear high and low sounds, loud and soft sounds. Some sounds are musical, and some sounds are just a big noise!

My ears catch the sounds from the air and take them through my ears to my **eardrums**. Next, the sound moves along three little bones (middle ear). Then it moves to a part that looks like a curly snail shell (inner ear) to reach nerves. The nerves take information about the sound on to my brain. Then I can hear the sound. This all happens very quickly.

7

List 5 sounds you can hear right now:

1. _____

2. _____

3. _____

4. _____

5. _____

8

My Sense of Sight

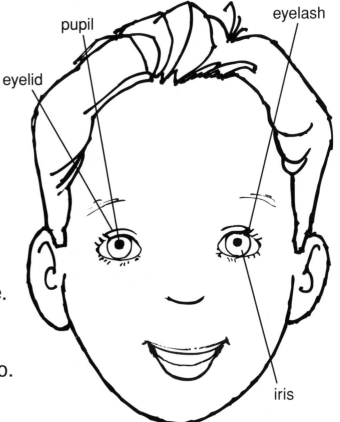

My eyes are round like balls.
Bones around my eyeballs
protect them.

The colored part is called the **iris**,
and the black part in the center
of the iris is called the **pupil**.

I have **eyelids** that open and close.
My eyelids and **eyelashes** help
deep dust out of my eyes.
Tears help to keep the dust out, too.

9

Light comes through an opening in my eye. It is called the **pupil**. The light then passes through the **lens**. The lens helps the light hit nerves at the back of my eyeball. The nerves carry a message to my brain. Then I can see. This all happens quickly.

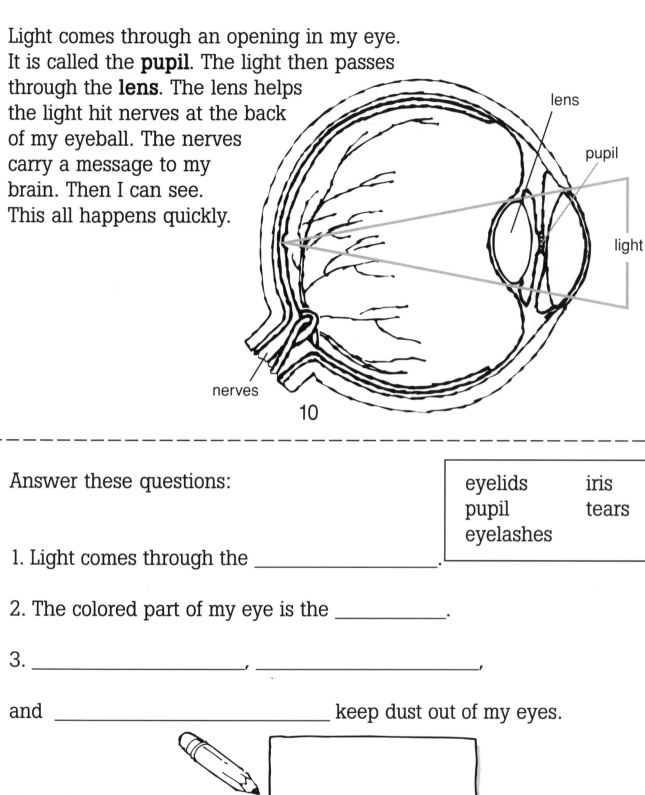

lens

pupil

light

nerves

10

Answer these questions:

eyelids	iris
pupil	tears
eyelashes	

1. Light comes through the _____.

2. The colored part of my eye is the _____.

3. _____, _____,

and _____ keep dust out of my eyes.

Draw the outside of one of your eyes here. What color is the iris? Label the parts.

Name_____

Which Senses Do I Use?

Name_____

What Am I?

Draw the answer.

I help you see.	I help you tell if something is hot, cold, wet, or sticky.	I can tell you what sound has been made.
You can smell a flower with me.	I can tell you if something is sweet or salty.	You use me to read a book.

Draw:
eyes
nose
mouth and tongue
ears
brain
hands

How Your Body Works • EMC 856

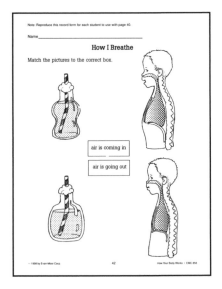

Watching Your Breathing

Have students sit quietly and feel the air moving in and out of their noses as they breathe. Have them place their hands on their chests to feel what happens as they breathe in and out. Ask students to explain what they think is happening.

A Respiration Experiment

Divide the class into small groups for the following experiment to model respiration. (Or demonstrate the experiment for the whole class.)

Each item in this experiment represents part of the respiratory system.

straw = windpipe	clay = throat
bottle = chest	water = air

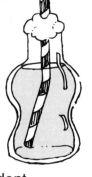

Materials (for each group)

- squeezable plastic bottle
- some clay
- straw
- water
- shallow tray (to catch spills)
- record sheet on page 42, reproduced for each student

Steps to Follow

1. Prepare the bottles.
   a. Fill the bottles almost to the top with water.
   b. Stick in the straw.
   c. Put clay around the opening so no air gets in that way.
2. Have students push in on the plastic bottle. Observe what happens to the water.
3. Have students stop pushing in on the bottle.

Follow Up

- Discuss what happened. *(When you push on the bottle it gets smaller, and the water pushes out. When you stop pushing in on the bottle, it gets bigger, and the water rushes back in.)* Ask, "How is this like what happens when you breathe?" *(When I make my chest big, air comes in. When I make my chest small, air goes out.)*
- Have students complete page 42 and then write a page for the class log together.

When I Breathe

Air comes in my nose.

It goes down a pipe to my lungs.

Then the air comes back out.

Gather More Information

- Show a video on respiration or read books such as *Breathing* by John Gaskin (Franklin Watts, 1984) and sections from *The Respiration System* by Dr. Virginia Alvin and Robert Silverstein (Twenty-First Century Books, 1994). Ask students to explain what they discovered about breathing.

- Reproduce a copy of the mini-book on pages 44–46 for each student, and make an overhead transparency of page 43. Use these to review how breathing occurs.

Read the mini-book with your students to verify what they discovered about breathing. Then show the transparency. Point to each part of the respiratory system. Ask students to name each part and describe its role in breathing. Make additions and corrections to both the class and individual logs.

Extension Activity—How Do You Talk?

Help students to understand the movement of air in and out of the throat, as needed for speech.

1. Pass out a balloon to each student. Tell them to blow up the balloons and hold the end so the air can't escape.
2. When everyone is ready, tell the students to make their balloons "talk."
3. Ask, "How are you able to make sounds with your balloon?" Listen to their explanations. Then explain that the air moving out of the balloon causes it to vibrate (move back and forth quickly). These vibrations cause the sound. Explain that there is a place in the throat called the vocal cords. When air from the lungs moves over the vocal cords, they vibrate making sounds. Our teeth, lips, and tongue help shape these vibrations into words.

Name _____

How I Breathe

Match the pictures to the correct box.

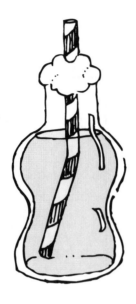

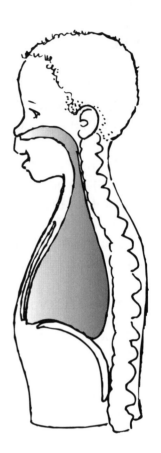

air is coming in

air is going out

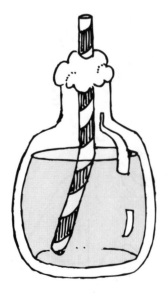

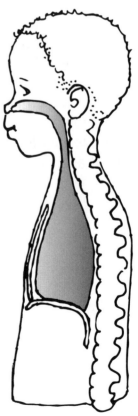

My Respiratory System

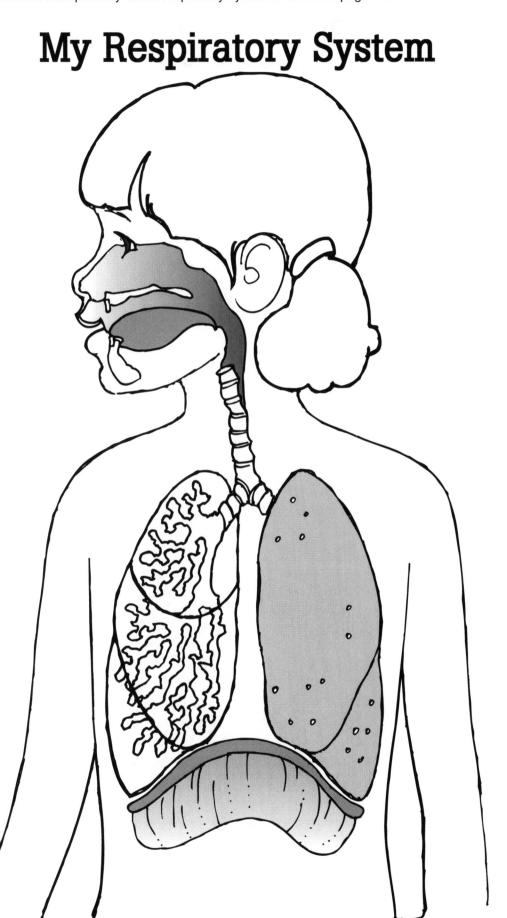

How Your Body Works • EMC 856

How Do I Get Oxygen?
(Respiration)

My body needs a special kind of gas called **oxygen**. Oxygen is in air. I get oxygen when I breathe.

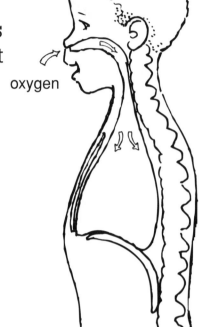

oxygen

1

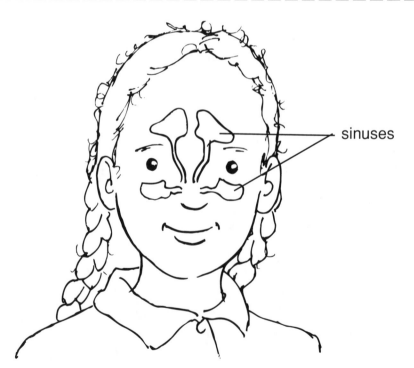

sinuses

I breathe air in through my nose. Hairs and sticky mucus inside my nose keep the dust and dirt from getting into my lungs. Spaces in my head called **sinuses** make the air wet and warm.

2

Air goes down my **windpipe** (trachea).
My windpipe has smaller branches that
end in my **lungs**. Oxygen is taken into
my lungs when I breathe in.

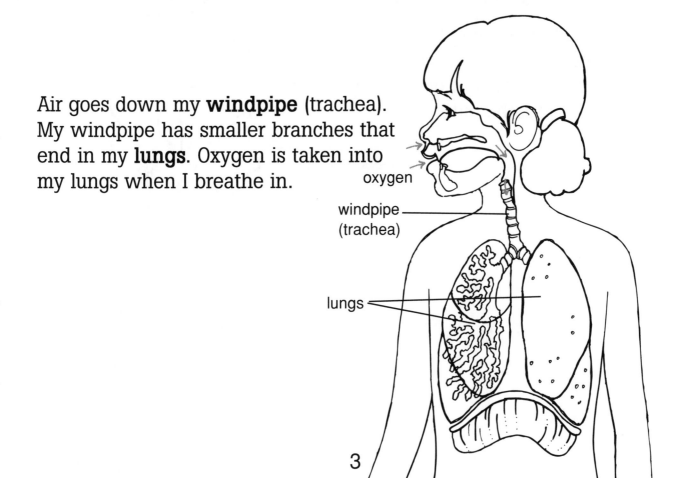

oxygen

windpipe
(trachea)

lungs

3

My lungs don't have muscles. I breathe by changing the size of
my chest. When I **inhale** (make my chest bigger), air comes into
my body.

When I **exhale** (make
my chest smaller), air is
pushed out. This is breathing.
I keep breathing even when
I am asleep.

4

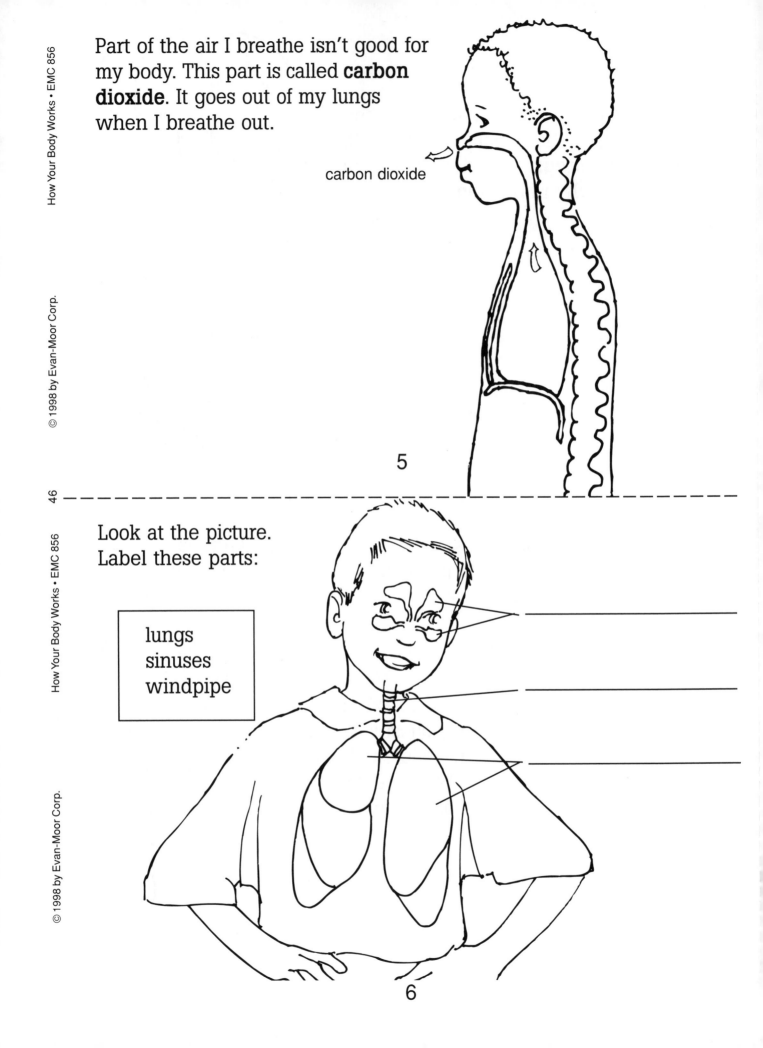

Part of the air I breathe isn't good for my body. This part is called **carbon dioxide**. It goes out of my lungs when I breathe out.

carbon dioxide

5

Look at the picture.
Label these parts:

lungs
sinuses
windpipe

6

The body digests food for energy.

Why Do We Need Food?

Engage students in a discussion of the food they ate for breakfast.
Ask students to explain why we need to eat food. Record their ideas
in the class log on a page entitled "We Need Food."

What Happens to the Food We Eat?

Read sections from *What Happens to a Hamburger?* by Paul Showers
(Thomas Y. Crowell, 1985). Then do the following demonstration to
illustrate part of the digestive process.

Materials

- apple slices (one for each student and some to put in blender)
- blender
- glass of water

Steps to Follow

1. Direct students to chew, but not swallow, their apple slices as you count to 20. After students
   swallow, talk about what happens to food in the mouth. *(Food gets smaller and mixes with saliva.
   As you continue to chew, the food gets even smaller and more mushy.)*
2. Put apple pieces in the blender. Pulse it to cut the apple into smaller chunks. Add a little water.
   Ask students to explain how this is like what happened to the apple in their mouth.
3. Blend the apple until it is mushy. Ask students to tell what part of the body (stomach) turns their
   food into mush. Ask what they think happens to the food next.

Follow Up

- Write a page entitled "What Happens to Our Food?" for the
  class log. Have students write about digestion in their individual
  logs, using the form on page 4.

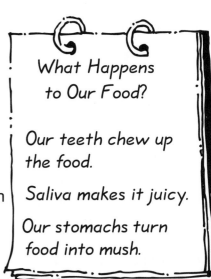

What Happens
to Our Food?

Our teeth chew up
the food.

Saliva makes it juicy.

Our stomachs turn
food into mush.

- Show a video or filmstrip on digestion or read sections from
  The Magic School Bus Inside the Human Body by Joanna Cole
  (Scholastic Inc., 1989). Have students use their new knowledge
  to check the information in the class log. It is important to make
  sure students understand that by the time food mixes with oxygen
  to provide energy, it is broken down into pieces too small to see.

Food to Energy

- Reproduce the digestion mini-book on pages 49–51 for each student. Read it together and have students complete the questions as a final check of student understanding of digestion.

- Make an overhead transparency of page 52. Use the transparency to point to areas as you discuss and list the steps in digesting food. List these steps on the chalkboard.

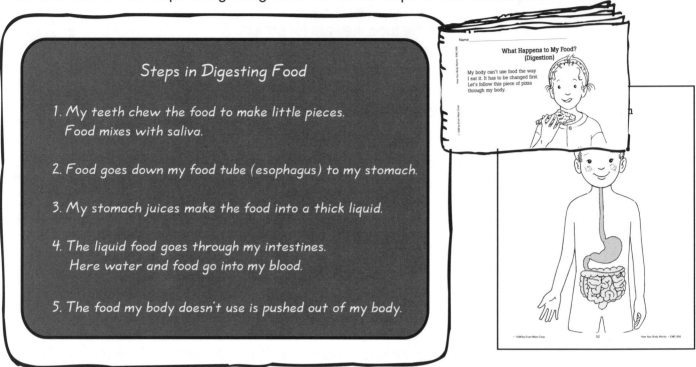

Steps in Digesting Food

1. My teeth chew the food to make little pieces. Food mixes with saliva.

2. Food goes down my food tube (esophagus) to my stomach.

3. My stomach juices make the food into a thick liquid.

4. The liquid food goes through my intestines. Here water and food go into my blood.

5. The food my body doesn't use is pushed out of my body.

- Have students copy the steps in their individual logs and make additions and changes to the class log.

- Make an overhead transparency of page 53 to show students as you explain how we get the energy to play and work.

How Long Are Your Intestines?

Students are always fascinated by how much intestine is wound up in their abdomens. Use adding machine tape to measure out the length of the intestines (averages about 23 feet or 7 meters).

Getting Rid of the Bad "Stuff"

- Review mini-book information about what happens to any food that isn't used by the body. Ask if there is anything else the body gets rid of. (You will get answers such as, *"Yellow stuff goes in the toilet. We go number 1. We pee."*) Explain that both kinds of waste have names—feces and urine.

- Reproduce the information on page 54 for each student. Use this page together to help students understand the ways our bodies get rid of harmful substances.

What Happens to My Food?
(Digestion)

My body can't use food the way I eat it. It has to be changed first. Let's follow this piece of pizza through my body.

I chew the pizza in my mouth. Chewing breaks the food into smaller pieces. **Saliva** (spit) mixes with the pizza and makes it softer.

2

I swallow and the pizza goes down my **food tube** (esophagus) and into my **stomach**. In my stomach, food is mixed all together. Stomach juices change the food into a thick liquid.

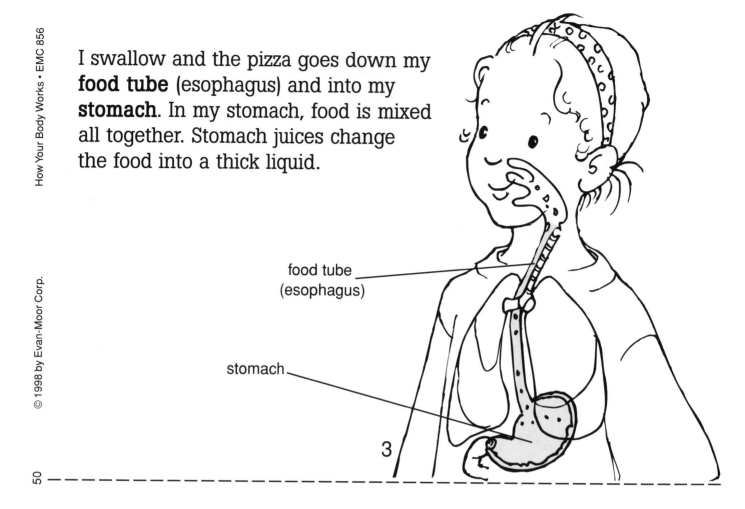

food tube
(esophagus)

stomach

3

The food moves to my **small intestines**. Here the digested food goes into my blood. The blood carries food all around my body. My body uses the food for energy.

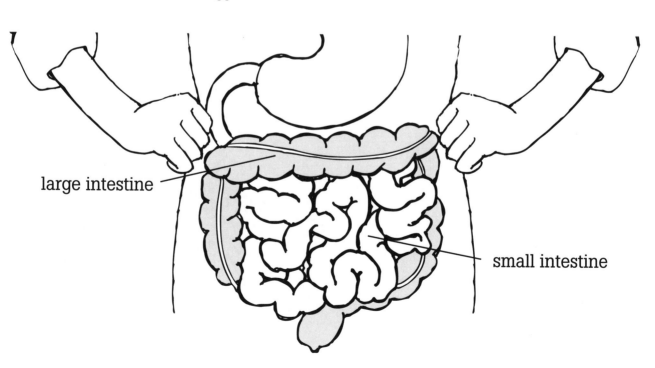

large intestine

small intestine

4

Some food is not used in my body. This is packed together in my **large intestine**.
When I go to the toilet, the waste is pushed out of my body.

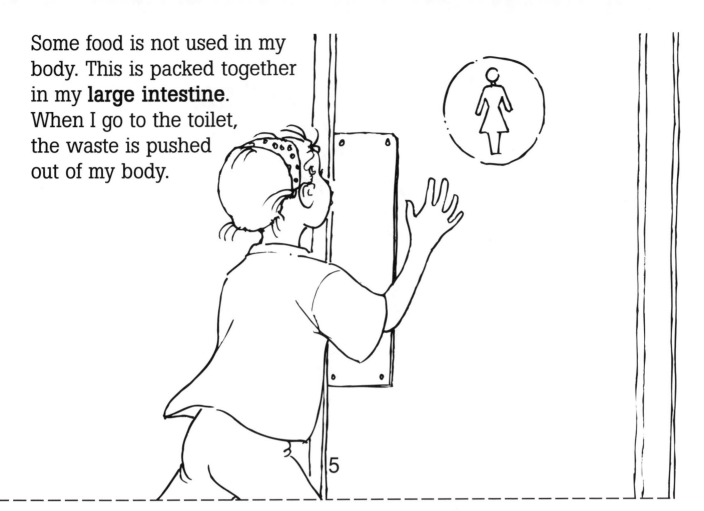

5

Where Does the Food Go?

Look at the picture. Read the words. Draw lines to match.

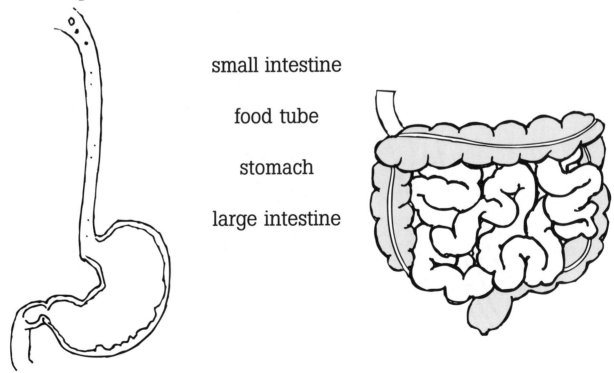

small intestine

food tube

stomach

large intestine

6

Note: Make an overhead transparency of the digestive tract to use with page 48.

Digestive System

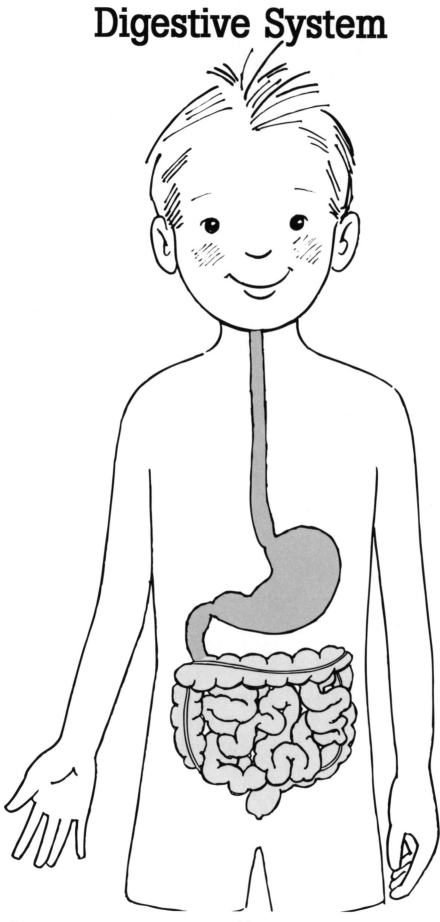

Note: Make an overhead transparency of this page to use with page 48.

Where Do You Get Your Energy?

Your body needs energy to move and think. The energy comes from mixing food and oxygen. This happens in all of the cells in your body.

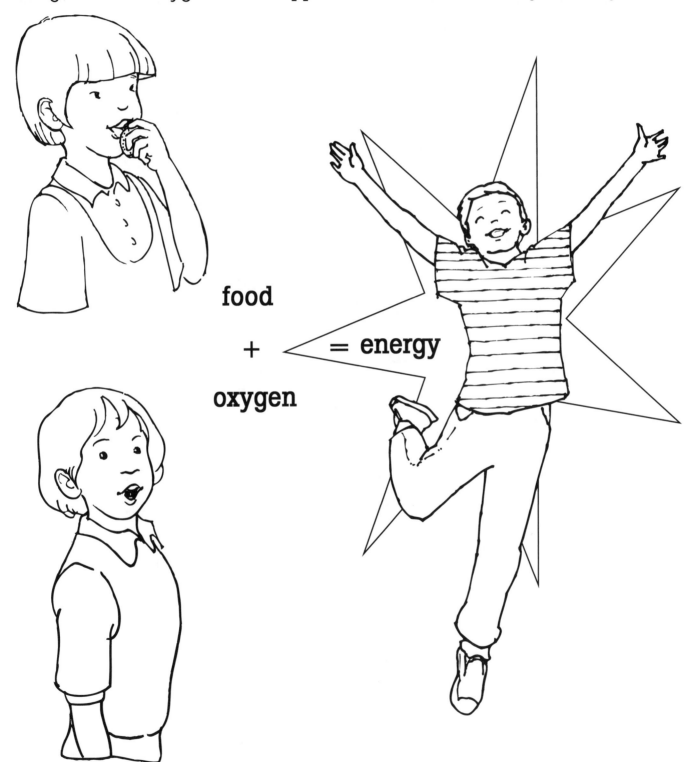

food

+

oxygen

= energy

Where do the food and oxygen come from?

 How Your Body Works • EMC 856

Name_____

Keeping the Inside of My Body Clean

Even if I eat only good foods and breathe clean air, my body will make some harmful wastes. My body gets rid of the waste in three ways.

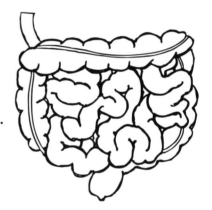

My lungs breathe out a gas called **carbon dioxide**. It is made when food is mixed with oxygen to make energy for my body.

Part of the food I eat is not used by my body. It is removed when I use the toilet. The solid brown material is called **feces** (fee-seez).

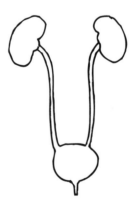

A special part of my body called **kidneys** take other wastes from my body. This is the yellow liquid called **urine** (yer-in) that I get rid of when I use the toilet.

Write the names of the three kinds of waste your body gets rid of:

_____ _____ _____

54

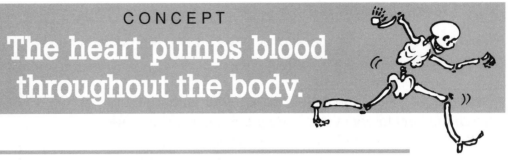

The heart pumps blood throughout the body.

Listen to Your Heart

Bring in a stethoscope. Name it and explain how it is used. Let everyone listen to his or her own heartbeat and the heartbeat of a classmate. (Clean the earpieces using a paper towel and rubbing alcohol before each use.)

How a Heart Works

• Share a video such as *The Heart and How it Works* (Our Wonderful Body Series; Coronet, 1992) or read sections about the heart and circulation from library books. Ask students to listen carefully to discover the job of the heart and the job of the blood vessels.

• After reading one or more selections, write information learned on a page entitled "My Heart" for the class log.

> *My Heart*
>
> *It pumps blood through little tubes.*
>
> *Blood takes food to my body.*
>
> *Blood takes oxygen to my body.*

Count Your Heart Beat

Before beginning this activity, reproduce the record sheet on page 57 for each student.

1. Demonstrate how to find a pulse on the left side of the neck. Have students practice until all are able to feel the pulse and count accurately.

2. Have students count their pulses for one minute while sitting. Say, "Start counting when I say go. Stop when I say stop."

3. Ask students to tell how many beats they counted. Have them record the number on their record sheets.

4. Ask, "Does your heart beat the same all the time?" Have students discover the answer by checking their pulses after doing the following activities. Discuss the results and have students complete the record sheets.
    a. Count after standing up for 1 minute.
    b. Count after jumping up and down for 1 minute.

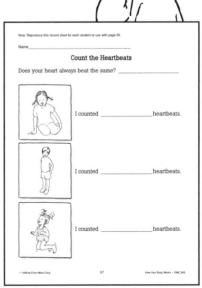

Gather More Information

- Make an overhead transparency of page 58 and reproduce a copy of the "Circulation" mini-book on pages 59–61 for each student.

  Read pages 1–4 of the mini-book together to learn more about the circulatory system. (Pages 5 and 6 will be used with "The Parts of the Blood.") Then show the transparency. Point to each part of the circulatory system. Ask students to name the part and describe what happens there. Make any additions or corrections to the class log at this time.

- Bring in an animal heart (ask your butcher for a calf heart) or borrow a heart model from a high school science department. Use it to show the chambers of the heart, the valves, and where the arteries and veins enter and leave the heart.

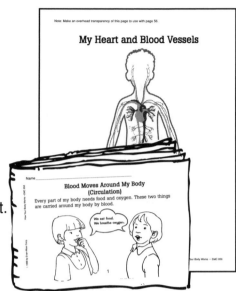

The Parts of Blood

Your students have learned that the heart pumps blood around the body. They have learned that the blood carries oxygen and food to all parts of the body. Now introduce the different functions of the blood cells.

- Read pages 14–17 in *The Magic School Bus Inside the Human Body* by Joanna Cole (Scholastic Inc., 1989). Have students share what they discovered about blood from the story. Verify this information by reading pages 5 and 6 in the mini-book together.

- As a class, write a class log page entitled "Blood Cells." Have students write in their individual logs, using the form on page 4.

Putting It All Together

- Now that students have been introduced to the respiratory, digestive, and circulatory systems, review how the systems work together. (Blood carries oxygen and food around the body. The lungs and parts of the digestive system get rid of waste products.)

- Reproduce pages 62 and 63 for each student. They will cut out the pieces and glue them to the body shape.

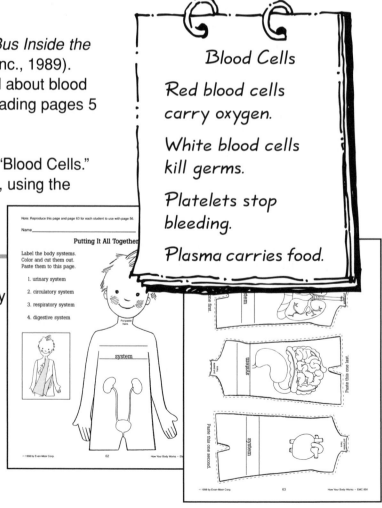

Note: Reproduce this record sheet for each student to use with page 55.

Name _____

Count the Heartbeats

Does your heart always beat the same? _____

I counted _____ heartbeats.

I counted _____ heartbeats.

I counted _____ heartbeats.

Note: Make an overhead transparency of this page to use with page 56.

My Heart and Blood Vessels

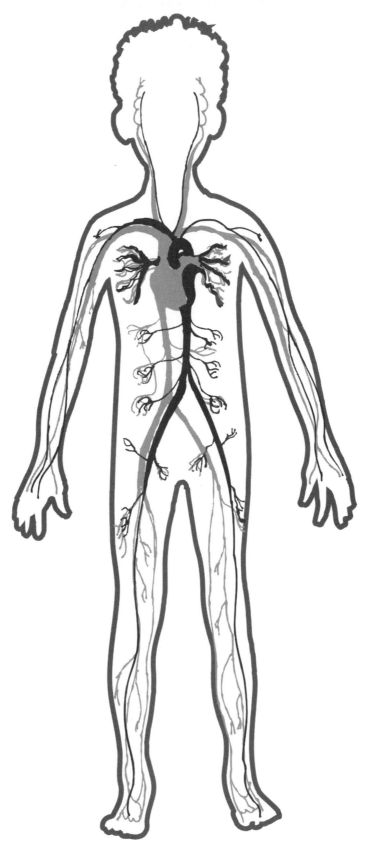

   How Your Body Works • EMC 856

Blood Moves Around My Body
(Circulation)

Every part of my body needs food and oxygen. These two things are carried around my body by blood.

We eat food.
We breathe oxygen.

1

My heart is a pump made of muscle. The beating of my heart makes the blood flow.

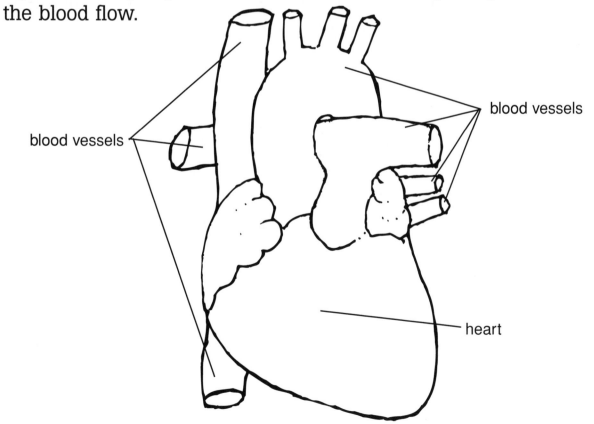

blood vessels

blood vessels

heart

2

My heart pumps blood through pipes called **blood vessels**.

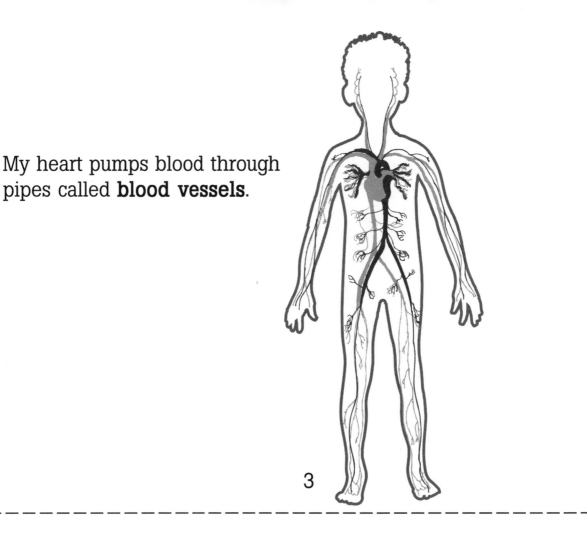

3

Arteries and veins are connected by tiny vessels called **capillaries**. Capillaries are so small, blood has to go through them one cell at a time.

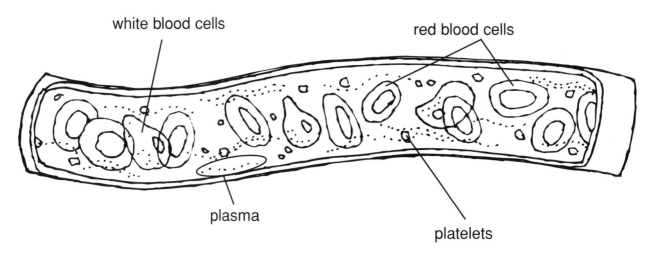

white blood cells

red blood cells

plasma

platelets

4

Blood has many parts.

Red blood cells carry oxygen.

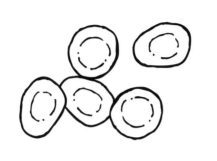

White blood cells fight germs.

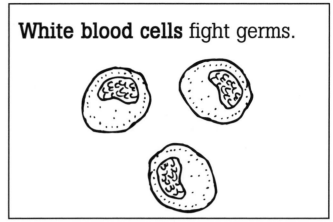

Plasma carries food.   **Platelets** help stop bleeding.

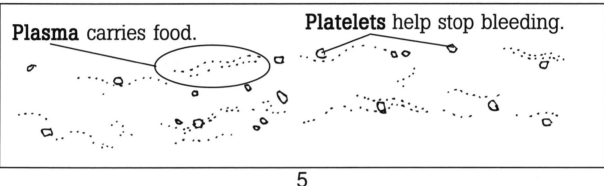

5

There are two kinds of blood vessels.

Arteries take fresh blood away from my heart.

Veins take used blood back to my heart.

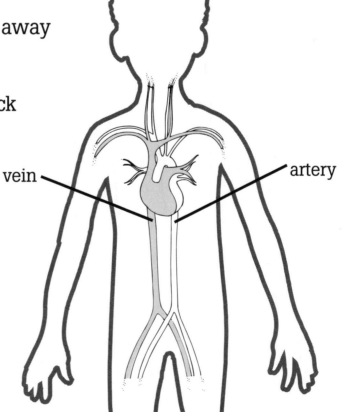

vein   artery

6

Note: Reproduce this page and page 63 for each student to use with page 56.

Name_____

Putting It All Together

Label the body systems.
Color and cut them out.
Paste them to this page.

1. urinary system

2. circulatory system

3. respiratory system

4. digestive system

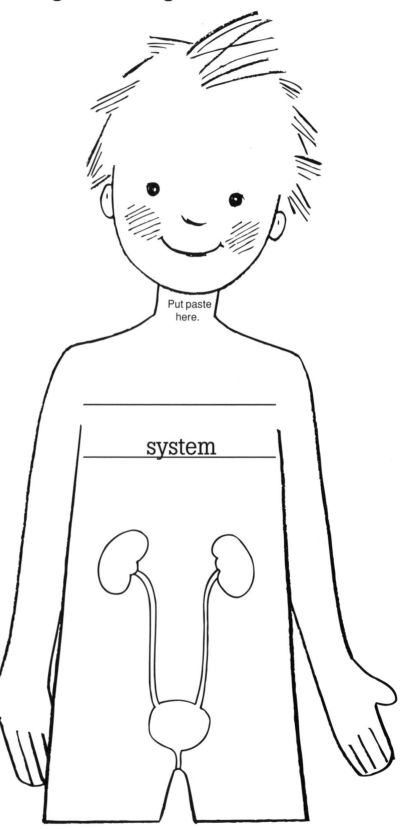

Put paste here.

_____

system

How Your Body Works • EMC 856

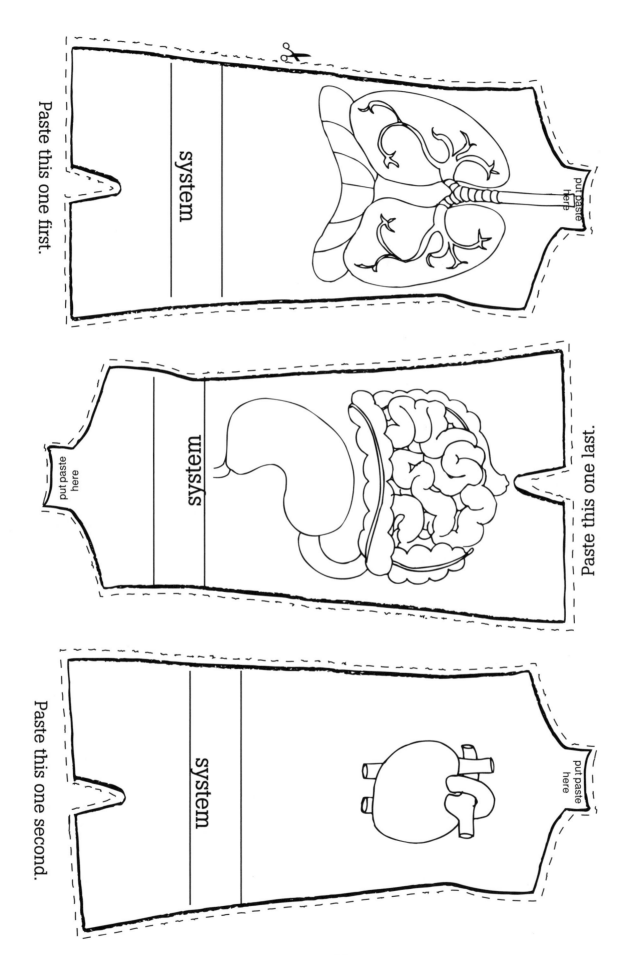

Paste this one first.

system

put paste
here

system

put paste
here

Paste this one last.

Paste this one second.

system

put paste
here

Bones support and help move the body.

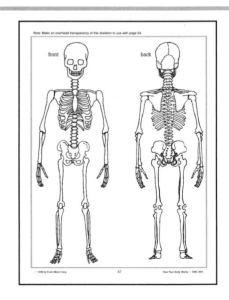

We Need Our Bones

- Use a bean bag animal to represent the body with no bones. Let several students try to figure out how to make it stand alone. (If someone props the bean bag up, explain that it isn't "standing on its own.") Ask them to explain why the animal keeps falling over. *(It's too soft. There is nothing in it to hold it up.)*

  Say, "You are all sitting up. What keeps you from falling over like the bean bag animal?" *(We have bones inside.)* Have students demonstrate how they would look if they had nothing inside to hold them up. After they collapse in their chairs or on the floor, ask them to try to move around without using their bones.

- Ask students to name some of the ways we use our bones. Record these in the class log on a page entitled "We Use Our Bones." Have students record what they have learned in their individual logs, using the form on page 4.

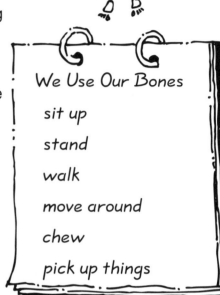

We Use Our Bones

sit up

stand

walk

move around

chew

pick up things

- Have students "feel" their bones. Give directions such as the following:
  "Feel your fingers and hand. Do you feel a few bones or a lot of bones?"
  "Touch the top and back of your head. Now touch your chin as you move your jaw."
  "Touch your chest. Can you find your rib bones?"

Gather More Information

Bones

- Read a book about skeletons, such as *The Skeleton Inside You* by Philip Balestrino (Thomas Y. Crowell, 1989), *Bones* by Anna Sandeman (Millbrook, 1995), or *Skeleton* by Steve Parker (Copper Beech Books, 1996).

- Ask students to tell what they learned about bones from the readings. Show a model of a skeleton or make an overhead transparency of the skeleton on page 67. Name common bones and ask students to find them on the model or the transparency. Then have everyone point to the part of their own body where that bone is found.

- Start a class log page entitled "My Skeleton." Have students write about skeletons in their individual logs, using the form on page 4.

- Reproduce page 68 for each student. Have students write the names of the bones on the correct lines. (You may need to make an overhead transparency of the page to use with younger students. They name the bone; you write the name; they copy it.)

My Skeleton

My body has many bones.

The bones are called a skeleton.

My skeleton helps me stand up and move.

Different bones have different names. Write the names of these bones on the lines.

- mandible
- rib cage
- vertebrae
- pelvis
- phalanges
- femur
- patella
- metatarsals

Word Box

arm bone	backbones
finger bones	foot bones
hipbone	jawbone
kneecap	ribs
skull	thigh bone

When I am grown up, I will have 206 bones.

Joints

- Have students bend their arms and legs and turn their heads. Ask them how these movements are possible. Provide the term "joints" if no one mentions it.

Explain that joints are where two bones come together. We have joints to allow us to move. There are different kinds of joints. While we can't see the different kinds of joints, we can see how they work. (You may want to introduce the terms "hinge" and "ball and socket" if appropriate.)

1. Say "You have joints that let you bend." Have students sit down and bend a leg at the knee. Have them move the leg up and down several times. Ask, "Where else do you have this kind of joint?" *(elbow)*
2. Say "You have joints that let you move in many directions." Have students put an arm straight out at the side without bending it at the elbow. Have them move the arm in a circle at the shoulder. Have them hold a leg out straight and move it at the hip.

- Add a page entitled "Joints" to the class log. Have the students write about joints for their individual logs, using the form on page 4.

My Skeleton Mini-book

Reproduce the mini-book on pages 69–72 for each student. Read and discuss the information together. Then make corrections and additions to both the class and individual logs.

Skeleton Puzzle

Materials

- pages 73 and 74, reproduced for each student
- piece of construction paper 12" x 18" (30.5 x 45.5 cm)
- scissors
- paste
- pencil

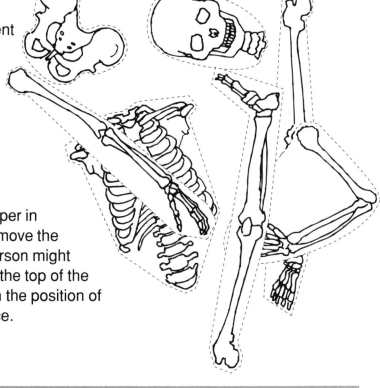

Steps to Follow

1. Students cut out all skeleton pieces.
2. They lay the pieces on the construction paper in the correct positions. (Encourage them to move the bones about to illustrate a movement a person might make—dancing, throwing a ball, touching the top of the skull with a hand, etc.) When satisfied with the position of the bones, students paste down each piece.
3. Have students label the major bones.

Bones Need Calcium

Bones need minerals to remain hard and strong. This experiment shows what happens to a bone without enough calcium.

Materials (for each group)

- chicken leg bone
- jar with lid
- vinegar
- logbook form on page 5, reproduced for each student

Steps to Follow

1. Have each group feel their bones. Have them record what they think will happen in their individual logs.
2. Students put the bone in the jar. They cover it with vinegar and put the lid on the jar.
3. They leave the bone in the vinegar for two weeks.
4. At the end of two weeks, students wash the bone and dry it.
5. Have them to try to bend the bone. Have them write what they observe in their individual logs.
6. Ask, "Why can you bend the bone?"

Explain that the vinegar took the minerals out of the bone. The minerals are what keep the bones hard. We get the mineral calcium from the foods we eat and drink.

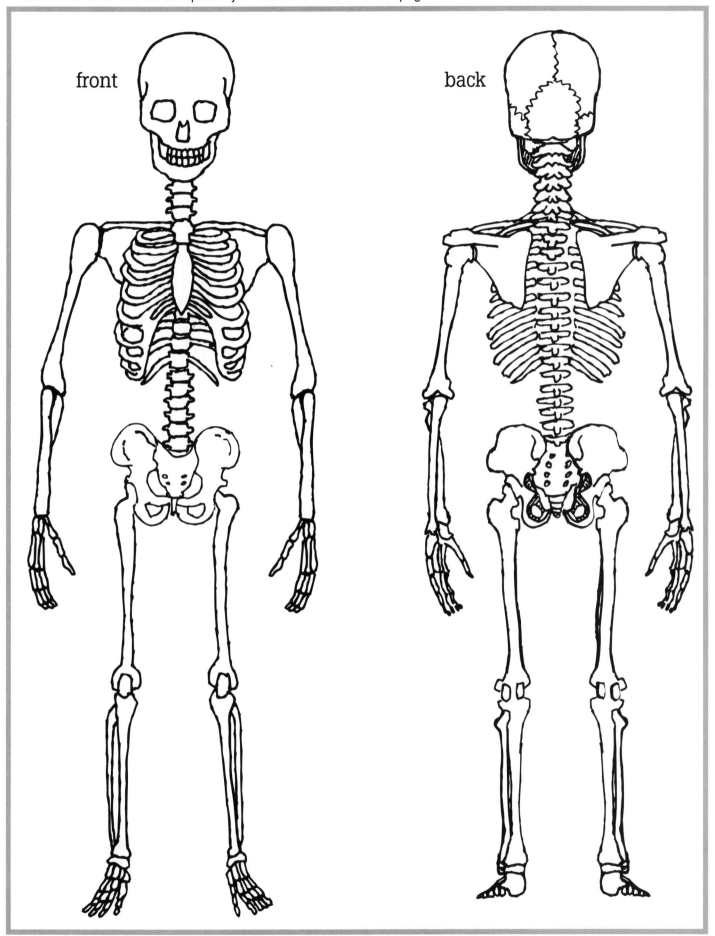

front

back

Name_____

Name the Bones

Different bones have different names. Write the names of these bones on the lines.

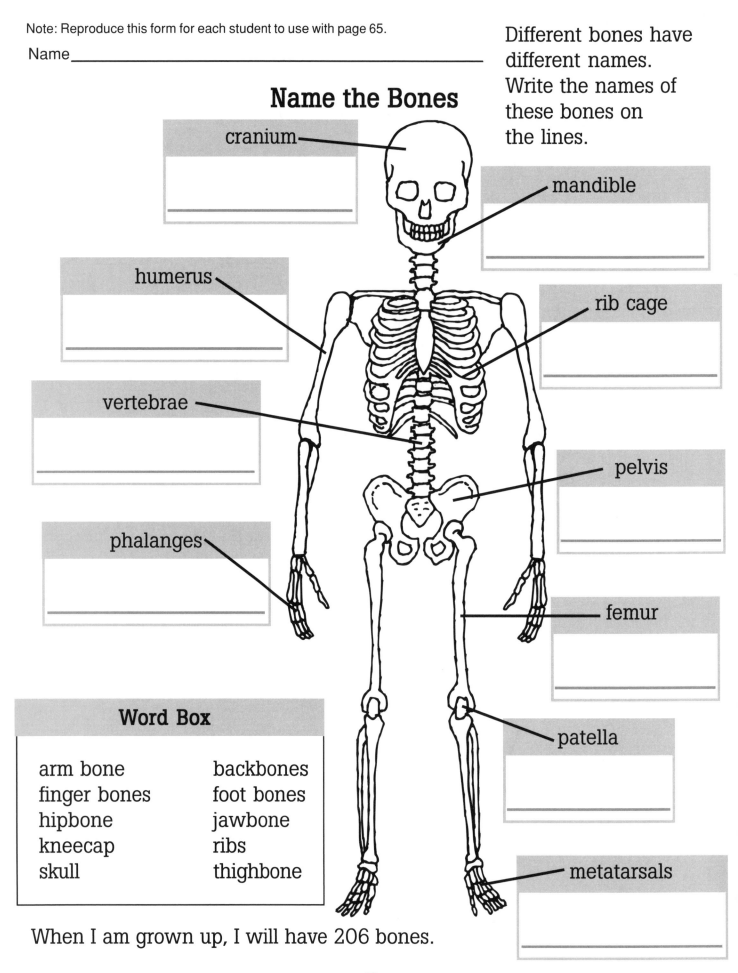

cranium

mandible

rib cage

humerus

vertebrae

pelvis

phalanges

femur

patella

metatarsals

Word Box

arm bone	backbones
finger bones	foot bones
hipbone	jawbone
kneecap	ribs
skull	thighbone

When I am grown up, I will have 206 bones.

How Your Body Works • EMC 856

My Skeleton

Fish, birds, frogs, cats, and snakes are like me in an important way. They all have bones. Bones help fish swim and birds fly. Bones help cats run and climb. They help frogs hop and snakes to slither. Bones help me run, jump, and stand up.

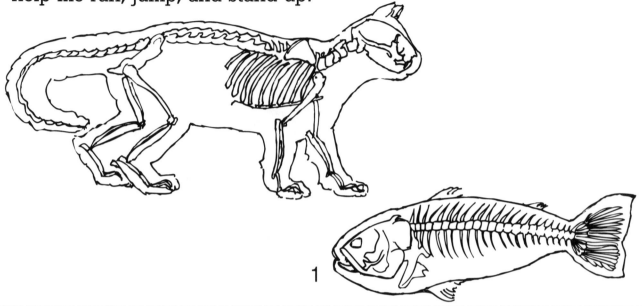

1

How Your Body Works • EMC 856

69

Answer these questions:

1. How are you like a fish, frog, or snake? _____

_____

2. How do bones help a snake? _____

_____

3. How do bones help you? _____

_____

My body has many bones. These bones are called a **skeleton**. My skeleton gives my body its shape and holds me up.

When I am all grown up, I will have 206 bones in my skeleton.

without
bones

with
bones

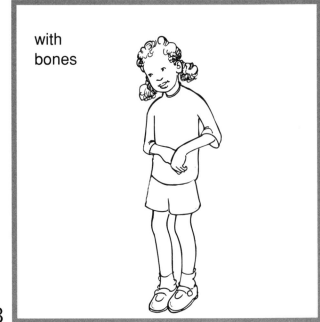

3

Fill in the blanks:

1. Bones _____ me up.

2. Bones give my body _____.

3. These bones are called a _____.

4

Some of the bones have special jobs.

The bones in the top of my **skull** protect my brain.

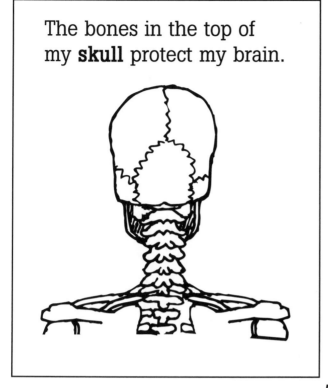

The bones in my **rib cage** protect my heart and lungs.

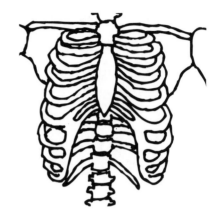

The bones in my **backbone** protect the nerves inside.

Bones can't bend. The **joints** in my body help me to bend, turn, and twist. There are joints where bones come together. **Ligaments** (bands like strong rubber bands) and **muscles** hold the bones together.

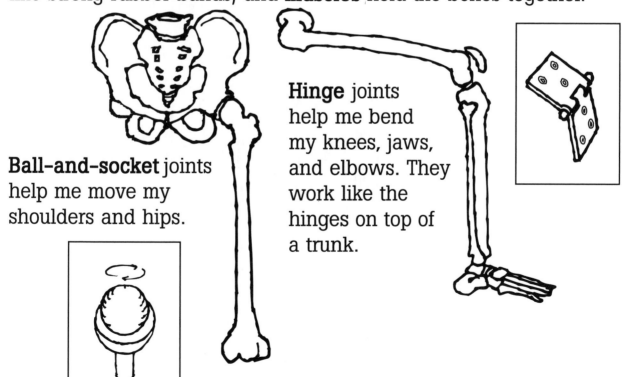

Ball-and-socket joints help me move my shoulders and hips.

Hinge joints help me bend my knees, jaws, and elbows. They work like the hinges on top of a trunk.

Bones can break if they are bent too far.
A doctor will make an x-ray to see
where the break is. The doctor
will fit the broken bone back
together. A cast is put on to
keep the bone from moving
while it is healing.

7

Many bones have special cells inside them that make new blood for
my body. Some bones store minerals that help my body work.

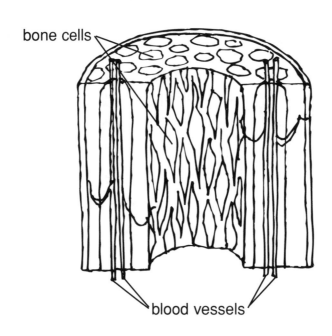

bone cells

blood vessels

8

Note: Reproduce the skeleton puzzle on this page and page 74 for each student to use with page 66.

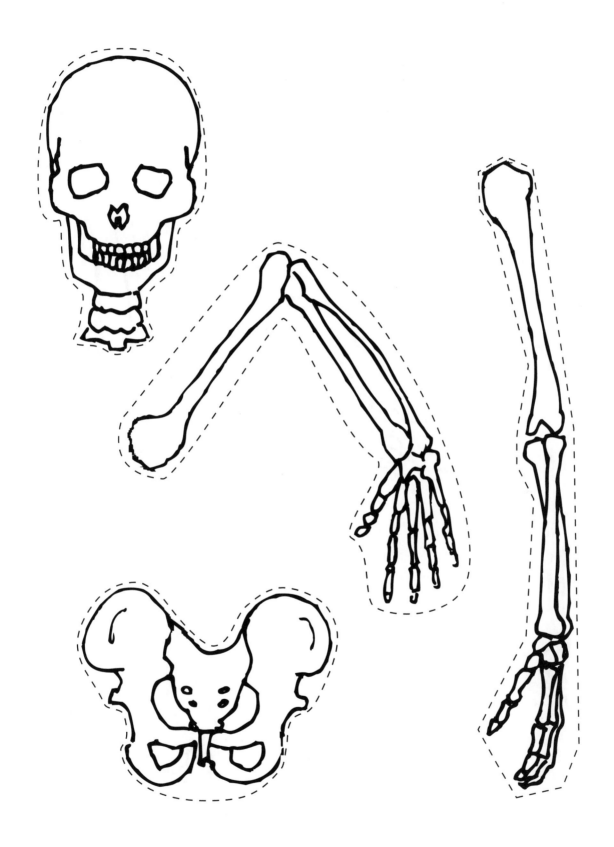

73

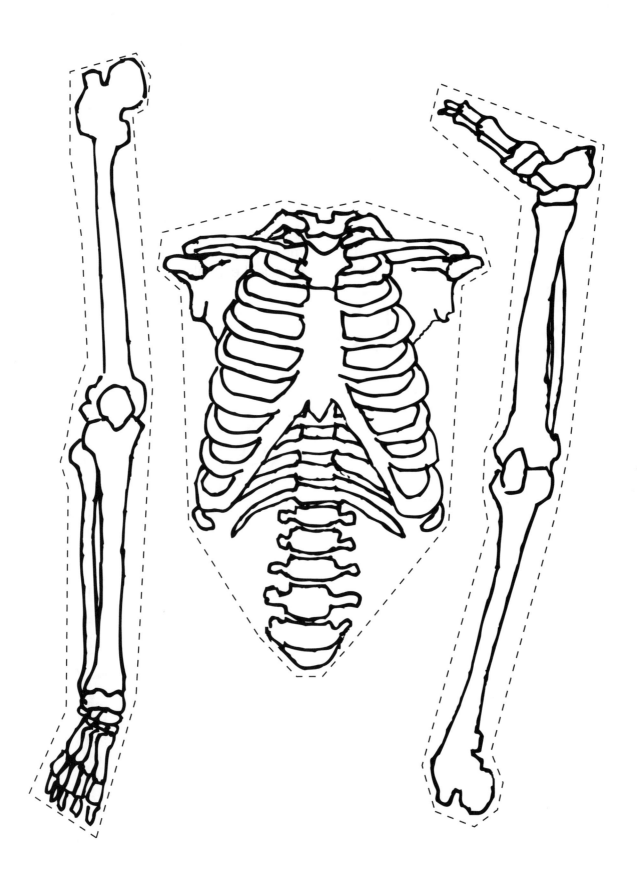

74

Muscles help the body move.

How Muscles Work

- Your students can't see their muscles, but they can feel them. Give the following directions:

  "Let your arm hang down. Feel your upper arm. Now make a muscle. What do you feel?"
  "Put your hands on your abdomen. Pull your muscles tight. Now relax. What do you feel?"
  "Put your hand around your calf. Tighten the muscle. Let it relax. What do you feel?"

  Explain that students will be learning about muscles and how they work.

- Read about muscles from reference books or check your district audiovisual catalog for a video or filmstrip on how muscles work.

- Make an overhead transparency of page 77.

  Display the overhead transparency as you review how a muscle works. Have the students look at the muscle in the arm that is working. Ask, "What is the muscle doing?" *(It's pulling.)* Then have them look at the muscle that is at rest. Ask, "What is that muscle doing?" *(It is relaxing.)*

- On the overhead, point to the spots where muscles are attached to bone. Explain that strong bands called tendons hold muscles to bones. Have students look at tendons on their bodies. Wiggle fingers to see the tendons in the back of the hand move. Feel the large tendon at the back of the ankle.

- Work with students to write a page entitled "Muscles" for the class log. Have students write about muscles in their individual logs, using the form on page 4.

- Reproduce the mini-book on pages 78–80 for each student. Read and complete the book together. Make any corrections or additions to the class log at this time.

Note: Make an overhead transparency of this form to use with page 75

How Muscles Work

Strong bands (tendons) hold the muscles to my bones. Nerves in the muscles take messages to my brain. These messages tell the muscles when to move and when to rest.

Muscles cannot push. They can only pull. Which muscles are pulling?

When a muscle relaxes, the bone or body part goes back to the first position. Which muscles are relaxing?

Muscles

Muscles help us run and play.

Muscles help us work.

Tendons hold our muscles to bones.

Muscles pull to work.

Muscles relax when work is done.

Name _____

My Muscles

I have more than 600 muscles in my body. Each muscle has a job to do. Without muscles I couldn't run, work, or play. Muscles help me wink, smile, bend, and kick a ball.

Extension Activities

Name the Parts

Explain that while we can't look directly at the muscles and tendons in our own bodies, we can use a chicken leg as a substitute.

Materials

- raw chicken legs (keep refrigerated or on ice until needed)
- pan
- adult (to supervise and assist)
- soap and paper towels (for clean up)
- logbook form on page 5, reproduced for each student

Steps to Follow

1. Divide the class into groups. Give each group a chicken leg.
2. Have students peel off the skin and look at the meat part (muscles).
3. They are to find where the muscles are attached to the bones (tendons).
4. Next they are to break open the bone (this must be done by an adult) to see what is inside.
5. Students return all parts of the chicken leg to the teacher in its pan.
6. Supervise the thorough washing of hands with soap and water.
7. Together, record the activity on the logbook form.

Keeping Strong

Explain that muscles must be worked to stay strong. Have students list all the things they can do to build strong muscles. List these on the chalkboard. Have each student select one way to illustrate it for a class book called "Keeping Strong." Select one student to create a cover for the book.

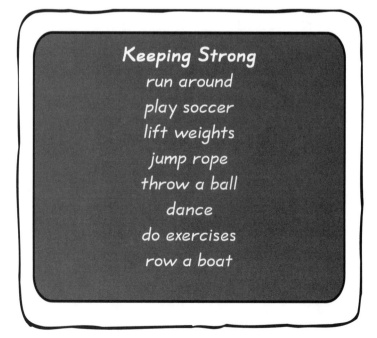

Keeping Strong

run around
play soccer
lift weights
jump rope
throw a ball
dance
do exercises
row a boat

Note: Make an overhead transparency of this page to use with page 75.

How Muscles Work

Strong bands (tendons) hold the muscles to my bones. Nerves in the muscles take messages to my brain. These messages tell the muscles when to move and when to rest.

Muscles cannot push. They can only pull. Which muscles are pulling?

When a muscle relaxes, the bone or body part goes back to the first position. Which muscles are relaxing?

My Muscles

I have more than 600 muscles in my body. Each muscle has a job to do. Without muscles I couldn't run, work, or play. Muscles help me wink, smile, bend, and kick a ball.

1

Muscles move the bones in my skeleton. They move food and blood around my body. They help my lungs to breathe and my heart to beat. When any part of my body moves, my muscles are working.

pull

relax

2

Strong bands called **tendons** hold the muscle to my bones.

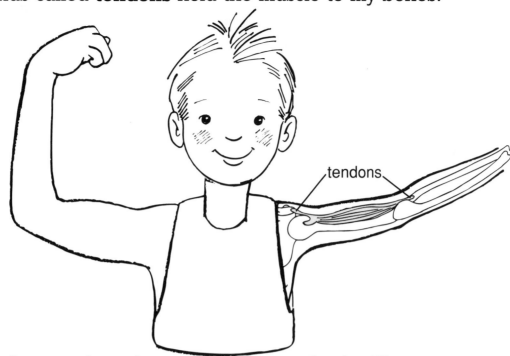

tendons

Nerves in the muscles take messages to my **brain**. These messages tell the muscles when to move and when to rest.

3

Color the bones yellow.
Color the muscles red.
Color the tendons blue.

Write the name of each part in the boxes.

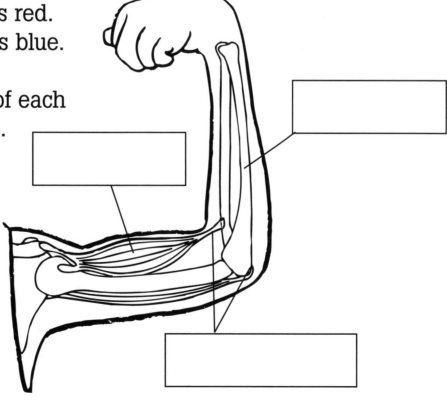

4

Muscles cannot push. They can only pull. When a muscle gets shorter, it pulls the bone or body part into a new position.

When the muscle relaxes, the bone or body part goes back to its first position.

Put an **X** on the muscles that are pulling.
Put a check on the muscles that are relaxed.

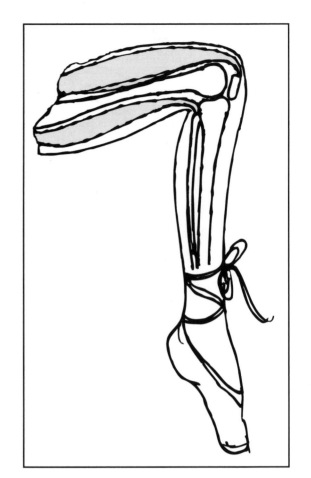

5

I can keep my muscles strong by getting healthy exercise.

6